RESURRECTION

by NEVILLE

•

PRAYER — THE ART OF BELIEVING

FEELING IS THE SECRET

FREEDOM FOR ALL

OUT OF THIS WORLD

RESURRECTION

•

 DEVORSS *Publications*

ISBN: 0-87516-076-X

Twelfth Printing, 1998

DeVorss & Company, Publisher
P.O. Box 550
Marina del Rey, CA 90294

Printed in The United States of America

CONTENTS

•

P R A Y E R
THE ART OF BELIEVING

N E V I L L E

PREFACE

PRAYER is the master key. A key may fit
one door of a house, but when it fits all
doors it may well claim to be a master key.
Such and no less a key is prayer to all
earthly problems.

1. *Law of Reversibility*

"Pray for my soul, more things are wrought by prayer than this world dreams of" (Tennyson).

PRAYER is an art and requires practice. The first requirement is a controlled imagination. Parade and vain repetitions are foreign to prayer. Its exercise requires tranquillity and peace of mind. "Use not vain repetitions," for prayer is done in secret and "thy Father which seeth in secret shall reward thee openly." The ceremonies that are customarily used in prayer are mere superstitions and have been invented to give prayer an air of solemnity. Those who do practice the art of prayer are often ignorant of the laws that control it. They attribute the results obtained to the ceremonies and mistake the letter for the spirit. The essence of prayer is faith; but faith must be permeated with understanding to be given that active quality which it does not possess when standing alone. "Therefore, get wisdom; and with all thy getting get understanding."

This book is an attempt to reduce the unknown to the known, by pointing out the conditions on which prayers are answered, and without which they cannot be answered. It defines the conditions governing prayer in laws that are simply a generalization of our observations.

The universal law of reversibility is the foundation on which its claims are based.

Mechanical motion caused by speech

was known for a long time before any one dreamed of the possibility of an inverse transformation, that is, the reproduction of speech by mechanical motion (the phonograph). For a long time electricity was produced by friction without ever a thought that friction, in turn, could be produced by electricity. Whether or not man succeeds in reversing the transformation of a force, he knows, nevertheless, that all transformations of force *are* reversible. If heat can produce mechanical motion, so mechanical motion can produce heat. If electricity produces magnetism, magnetism too can develop electric currents. If the voice can cause undulatory currents, so can such currents reproduce the voice, and so on. Cause and effect, energy and matter, action and reaction are the same and inter-convertible.

This law is of the highest importance, because it enables you to foresee the inverse transformation once the direct transformation is verified. If you knew how you would *feel* were you to realize your objective, then, inversely, you would know what state. you could realize were you to awaken in yourself such feeling. The injunction, to pray believing that you already possess what you pray for, is based upon a knowledge of the law of inverse transformation. If your realized prayer produces in you a definite feeling or state of consciousness, then, inversely, that particular feeling or state of consciousness *must* produce your realized prayer. Because all transformations of force are reversible, you should always assume the

4

feeling of your fulfilled wish. You should awaken within you the *feeling* that you are and have that which heretofore you desired to be and possess. This is easily done by contemplating the joy that would be yours were your objective an accomplished fact, so that you live and move and have your being in the feeling that your wish *is* realized.

The feeling of the wish fulfilled, if assumed and sustained, must objectify the state that would have created it. This law explains why "Faith is the substance of things hoped for, the evidence of things not seen" and why "He calleth things that are not seen *as though they were* and things that were not seen become seen." Assume the feeling of your wish fulfilled and continue feeling that it *is* fulfilled

5

until that which you feel objectifies itself.

If a physical fact can produce a psychological state, a psychological state can produce a physical fact. If the effect (a) can be produced by the cause (b), then inversely, the effect (b) can be produced by the cause (a). Therefore I say unto you, "What things soever ye desire, when ye pray, believe that ye have received them, and ye shall have them" (Mark 11:24, E. R. V.).

2. *Dual Nature of Consciousness*

A clear concept of the dual nature of
man's consciousness must be the basis of
all true prayer. Consciousness includes a
subconscious as well as a conscious part.
The infinitely greater part of consciousness lies below the sphere of objective
consciousness. The subconscious is the
most important part of consciousness. It
is the cause of voluntary action. The subconscious is what a man *is*. The conscious
is what a man *knows*. "I and my Father
are one but my Father is greater than I."
The conscious and subconscious are one,
but the subconscious is greater than the
conscious.

"I of myself can do nothing, the Father
within me He doeth the work." I, ob-

7

jective consciousness, of myself can do nothing; the Father, the subconscious, He doeth the work. The subconscious is that in which everything is known, in which everything is possible, to which everything goes, from which everything comes, which belongs to all, to which all have access.

What we are conscious of is constructed out of what we are not conscious of. Not only do our subconscious assumptions influence our behavior but they also fashion the pattern of our objective existence. They alone have the power to say, "Let us make man—objective manifestations—in our image, after our likeness." The whole of creation is alseep within the deep of man and is awakened to objective existence by his subconscious assumptions.

Within that blankness we call sleep there is a consciousness in unsleeping vigilance, and while the body sleeps this unsleeping being releases from the treasure house of eternity the subconscious assumptions of man.

Prayer is the key which unlocks the infinite storehouse. "Prove me now herewith, saith the Lord of hosts, if I will not open you the windows of heaven, and pour you out a blessing, that there shall not be room enough to receive it." Prayer modifies or completely changes our subconscious assumptions, and a change of assumption is a change of expression.

The conscious mind reasons inductively from observation, experience and education. It therefore finds it difficult to believe what the five senses and inductive reason deny. The subconscious reasons deductively and is never concerned with the truth or falsity of the premise, but proceeds on the assumption of the correctness of the premise and objectifies results which are consistent with the premise. This distinction must be clearly seen by all who would master the art of praying. No true grasp of the science of prayer can be really obtained until the laws governing the dual nature of consciousness are understood and the importance of the subconscious realized.

Prayer—the art of believing what is denied by the senses—deals almost entirely with the subconscious. Through prayer, the subconscious is suggested into acceptance of the wish fulfilled, and, reasoning deductively, logically unfolds it to its legitimate end. "Far greater is He that is in you than he that is in the world."

The subjective mind is the diffused consciousness that animates the world; it is the spirit that giveth life. In all substance is a single soul—subjective mind. Through all creation runs this one unbroken subjective mind. Thought and feeling fused into beliefs impress modifications upon it, charge it with a mission, which mission it faithfully executes.

The conscious mind originates premises. The subjective mind unfolds them to their logical ends. Were the subjective mind not so limited in its initiative power of reasoning, objective man could not be held responsible for his actions in the world. Man transmits ideas to the subconscious through his feelings. The subconscious transmits ideas from mind to mind through telepathy. Your unexpressed convictions of others are transmitted to them without their conscious knowledge or consent, and if subconsciously accepted by them will influence their behavior.

The only ideas they subconsciously reject are your ideas of them which they could not wish to be true of anyone. Whatever they could wish for others can be believed of them, and by the law of belief which governs subjective reasoning they are compelled to subjectively accept, and therefore objectively express, accordingly.

The subjective mind is completely controlled by suggestion. Ideas are best suggested when the objective mind is partly subjective, that is, when the objective senses are diminished or held in abeyance. This partly subjective state can best be described as *controlled reverie,* wherein the mind is passive but capable of functioning with absorption. It is a concentration of attention. There must be no conflict in your mind when you are praying. Turn from what *is* to what *ought to be.* Assume the mood of fulfilled desire, and by the universal law of reversibility you will realize your desire.

3. *Imagination and Faith*

PRAYERS are not successfully made unless there is rapport between the conscious and subconscious mind of the operator. This is done through imagination and faith.

By the power of imagination all men, certainly imaginative men, are forever casting forth enchantments, and all men, especially unimaginative men, are continually passing under their power. Can we ever be certain that it was not our mother while darning our socks who began that subtle change in our minds? If I can unintentionally cast an enchantment over persons, there is no reason to doubt that I am able to cast intentionally a far stronger enchantment.

14

IMAGINATION AND FAITH

Everything, that can be seen, touched, explained, argued over, is to the imaginative man nothing more than a means, for he functions, by reason of his controlled imagination, in the deep of himself where every idea exists in itself and not in relation to something else. In him there is no need for the restraints of reason, for the only restraint he can obey is the mysterious instinct that teaches him to eliminate all moods other than the mood of fulfilled desire.

Imagination and faith are the only faculties of mind needed to create objective conditions. The faith required for the successful operation of the law of consciousness is a purely subjective faith and is attainable upon the cessation of active opposition on the part of the objective mind of the operator. It depends upon your ability to feel and accept as true what your objective senses deny. Neither the passivity of the subject nor his conscious agreement with your suggestion is necessary, for without his consent or knowledge he can be given a subjective order which he must objectively express. It is a fundamental law of consciousness that by telepathy we can have immediate communion with another.

To establish rapport you call the subject mentally. Focus your attention on him and mentally shout his name just as you would to attract the attention of anyone. Imagine that he has answered, and mentally hear his voice. Represent him to yourself inwardly in the state you want him to obtain. Then imagine that he is telling you in the tones of ordinary conversation what you want to hear. Mentally answer him. Tell him of your joy in witnessing his good fortune. Having mentally heard with all the distinctness of reality that which you wanted to hear, and having thrilled to the news heard, return to objective consciousness. Your subjective conversation must awaken what it affirmed.

"Thou shalt decree a thing and it shall be established unto thee." It is not a strong will that sends the subjective word on its mission so much as it is clear thinking and feeling the truth of the state affirmed. When belief and will are in conflict, belief invariably wins. "Not by might, nor by power, but by my spirit, saith the Lord of hosts." It is not what

you want that you attract; you attract
what you believe to be true. Therefore,
get into the spirit of these mental conversations and give them the same degree of
reality that you would a telephone conversation. "If thou canst believe, all
things are possible to him that believeth.
Therefore, I say unto you, what things
soever ye desire, when ye pray, believe
that ye have received them, and ye shall
have them." The acceptance of the end
wills the means. And the wisest reflection could not devise more effective means
than those which are willed by the acceptance of the end. Mentally talk to your
friends as though your desires for them
were already realized.

Imagination is the beginning of the
growth of all forms, and faith is the sub-

stance out of which they are formed. By imagination, that which exists in latency or is asleep within the deep of consciousness is awakened and is given a form. The cures attributed to the influence of certain medicines, relics and places are the effects of imagination and faith. The curative power is not in the spirit that is in them, it is in the spirit in which they are accepted. "The letter killeth, but the spirit giveth life."

The subjective mind is completely controlled by suggestion, so, whether the object of your faith be true or false, you will get the same results. There is nothing unsound in the theory of medicine or in the claims of the priesthood for their relics and holy places. The subjective mind of the patient accepts the suggestion of health conditioned on such states, and as soon as these conditions are met proceeds to realize health. "According to your faith be it done unto you for all things are possible to him that believeth." Confident expectation of a state is the most potent means of bringing it about. The confident expectation of a cure does that which no medical treatment can accomplish.

Failure is always due to an antagonistic auto-suggestion by the patient, arising from objective doubt of the power of the medicine or relic, or from doubt of the truth of the theory. Many of us, either from too little emotion or too much intellect, both of which are stumbling blocks in the way of prayer, cannot believe that which our senses deny. To force ourselves to believe will end in greater doubt. To avoid such counter-suggestions the patient should be unaware, objectively, of the suggestions which are made to him. The most effective method of healing or influencing the behavior of others consists in what is known as "the silent or absent treatment." When the subject is unaware, objectively, of the suggestion given him there is no possibility of him setting up an antagonistic belief. It is not necessary that the patient know, objectively, that anything is being done for him. From what is known of the subjective and objective processes of reasoning, it is better that he should not know objectively of that which is being done for him. The more completely the objective mind is kept in ignorance of the suggestion, the better will the subjective mind perform its functions. The subject subconsciously accepts the suggestion and thinks he originates it, proving the truth of Spinoza's dictum that we know not the causes that determine our actions.

The subconscious mind is the universal conductor which the operator modifies with his thoughts and feelings. Visible states are either the vibratory effects of subconscious vibrations within you or they are the vibratory causes of corresponding vibrations within you. A disciplined man never permits them to be causes unless they awaken in him desirable states of consciousness. With a knowledge of the law of reversibility, the disciplined man transforms his world by imagining and feeling only what is lovely and of good report. The beautiful idea

he awakens within himself shall not fail
to arouse its affinity in others. He knows
the savior of the world is not a man but
the manifestation that would save. The
sick man's savior is health, the hungry
man's savior is food, the thirsty man's
savior is water. He walks in the company
of the savior by assuming the feeling of
his wish fulfilled. By the laws of reversibility, that all transformations of force
are reversible, the energy or feeling
awakened transforms itself into the state
imagined. He never waits four months
for the harvest. If in four months the
harvest will awaken in him a state of joy,
then, inversely, the joy of harvest *now* will
awaken the harvest now. "Now is the acceptable time to give beauty for ashes, joy
for mourning, praise for the spirit of

heaviness; that they might be called trees of righteousness, the planting of the Lord that he might be glorified."

4. *Controlled Reverie*

EVERYONE is amenable to the same psychological laws which govern the ordinary hypnotic subject. He is amenable to control by suggestion. In hypnosis, the objective senses are partly or totally suspended. However, no matter how profoundly the objective senses are locked in hypnosis, the subjective faculties are alert, and the subject recognizes everything that goes on around him. The activity and power of the subjective mind are proportionate to the sleep of the objective mind. Suggestions which appear powerless when presented directly to objective consciousness are highly efficacious when the subject is in the hypnotic state. The hypnotic state is simply being unaware, objectively. In hypnotism, the conscious mind is put to sleep and the subconscious powers are exposed so as to be directly reached by suggestion. It is easy to see from this, providing you accept the truth of mental suggestions, that any one not objectively aware of you is in a profound hypnotic state relative to you. Therefore, "Curse not the king, no not in thy thought; and curse not the rich in thy bedchamber; for a bird of the air shall carry the voice, and that which hath wings shall tell the matter" (Ecc. 10:20). What you sincerely believe as true of another you awaken within him.

No one need be entranced, in the ordinary manner, to be helped. If the subject is consciously unaware of the suggestion, and if the suggestion is given with conviction and confidently accepted by the operator as true, then you have the ideal setting for a successful prayer. Represent the subject to yourself mentally as though he had already done that which you desire him to do. Mentally speak to him and congratulate him on having done what you want him to do. Mentally see him in the state you want him to obtain. Within the circle of its action, every word subjectively spoken awakens, objectively, what it affirms. Incredulity on the part of the subject is no hindrance when you are in control of your reverie.

Bold assertion by you, while you are in a partly subjective state, awakens what you affirm. Self-confidence on your part and the thorough belief in the truth of your mental assertion are all that is needed to produce results. Visualize the subject and imagine that you hear his voice. This establishes contact with his subjective mind. Then imagine that he is telling you what you want to hear. If you want to send him words of health and wealth, then imagine that he is telling you, "I have never felt better and I have never had more," and mentally tell him of your joy in witnessing his good fortune. Imagine that you see and hear his joy.

A mental conversation with the subjective image of another must be in a manner which does not express the slightest doubt as to the truth of what you hear and say. If you have the least idea that you do not believe what you have imagined you have heard and seen, the subject will not comply, for your subjective mind will transmit only your fixed ideas. Only fixed ideas can awaken their vibratory correlates in those toward whom they are directed. In the controlled reverie, ideas must be suggested with the utmost care. If you do not control your imagination in the reverie, your imagination will control you. Whatever you suggest with confidence is law to the subjective mind; it is under obligation to objectify that which you mentally affirm. Not only does the subject execute the state affirmed but he does it as though the decision had come of itself, or the idea had been originated by him.

Control of the subconscious is dominion over all. Each state obeys one mind's control. Control of the subconscious is accomplished through control of your beliefs, which in turn is the all-potent factor in the production of visible states. Imagination and faith are the secrets of creation.

5. *Law of Thought Transmission*

"HE sent his word and healed them, and delivered them from their destructions." He transmitted the consciousness of health and it awoke its vibratory correlate in the one toward whom it was directed. He mentally represented the subject to himself in a state of health and imagined he heard the subject confirm it. "For no word of God shall be void of power; therefore hold fast the pattern of healthful words which thou hast heard."

To pray successfully you must have clearly defined objectives. You must know what you want before you can ask for it. You must know what you want before you can *feel* that you have it, and prayer is the feeling of fulfilled desire.

PRAYER

It does not matter what it is you seek in prayer, or where it is, or whom it concerns. You have nothing to do but convince yourself of the truth of that which you desire to see manifested. When you emerge from prayer you no longer seek, for you have—if you have prayed correctly—subconsciously assumed the reality of the state sought, and by the law of reversibility your subconscious assumption must objectify that which it affirms.

You must have a conductor to transmit a force. You may employ a wire, a jet of water, a current of air, a ray of light or any intermediary whatsoever. The principle of the photophone or the transmission of voice by light will help you to understand thought transmission, or the sending of a word to heal another. There is a strong analogy between a spoken voice and a mental voice. To think is to speak low, to speak is to think aloud. The principle of the photophone is this: A ray of light is reflected by a mirror and projected to a receiver at a distant point. Back of the mirror is a mouthpiece. By speaking into the mouthpiece you cause the mirror to vibrate. A vibrating mirror modifies the light reflected on it. The modified light has your speech to carry, not as speech, but as represented in its mechanical correlate. It reaches the distant station and impinges on a disk within the receiver; it causes the disk to vibrate according to the modification it undergoes —and it reproduces your voice.

"I am the light of the world." I am, the knowledge that I exist, is a light by means of which what passes in my mind is rendered visible. Memory, or my ability to mentally see what is not objectively present, proves that my mind is a mirror, and so sensitive a mirror that it can reflect a thought. The reperception of an image in memory in no way differs as a visual act from the perception of my image in a mirror. The same principle of seeing is involved in both.

Your consciousness is the light reflected on the mirror of your mind and projected in space to the one of whom you think. By mentally speaking to the subjective image in your mind you cause the mirror of your mind to vibrate. Your vibrating mind modifies the light of consciousness reflected on it. The modified light of consciousness reaches the one toward whom it is directed and impinges on the mirror of his mind; it causes his mind to vibrate according to the modifications it undergoes. Thus, it reproduces in him what was mentally affirmed by you.

Your beliefs, your fixed attitudes of mind, constantly modify your consciousness as it is reflected on the mirror of your mind. Your consciousness, modified by your beliefs, objectifies itself in the conditions of your world. To change the world, you must first change your conception of it. To change a man, you must change your conception of him. You must believe him to be the man you want him to be and mentally talk to him

as though he were. All men are suffi-
ciently sensitive to reproduce your beliefs
of them. Therefore, if your word is not
reproduced visibly in him toward whom
it is sent, the cause is to be found in you,
not in the subject. As soon as you
believe in the truth of the state affirmed,
results follow. Everyone can be transformed; every thought can be transmitted; every thought can be visibly
embodied.

Subjective words—subconscious assumptions—awaken what they affirm.
"They are living and active and shall not
return unto me void, but shall accomplish
that which I please, and shall prosper
in the thing whereto I sent them." They
are endowed with the intelligence per-
taining to their mission and will persist

until the object of their existence is realized; they persist until they awaken the vibratory correlates of themselves within the one toward whom they are directed, but the moment the object of their creation is accomplished they cease to be. The word spoken subjectively in quiet confidence will always awaken a corresponding state in the one for whom it was spoken; but the moment its task is accomplished it ceases to be, permitting the one in whom the state is realized to remain in the consciousness of the state affirmed or to return to his former state.

Whatever state has your attention holds your life. Therefore, to become attentive to a former state is to return to that condition. "Remember not the for-

mer things, neither consider the things of
old."

2.

Nothing can be added to man, for
the whole of creation is already perfected
within him. "The kingdom of heaven is
within you." "Man can receive nothing,
except it be given him from heaven."
Heaven is your subconsciousness. Not
even a sunburn is given from without.
The rays without only awaken corresponding rays within. Were the burning rays not contained within man, all
the concentrated rays in the universe
could not burn him. Were the tones of
health not contained within the consciousness of the one of whom they are affirmed,
they could not be vibrated by the word

which is sent. You do not really give to another—you resurrect that which is asleep within him. "The damsel is not dead, but sleepeth." Death is merely a sleeping and a forgetting. Age and decay are the sleep—not death—of youth and health. Recognition of a state vibrates or awakens it.

Distance, as it is cognized by your objective senses, does not exist for the subjective mind. "If I take the wings of the morning, and dwell in the uttermost parts of the sea; even there shall thy hand lead me." Time and space are conditions of thought; the imagination can transcend them and move in a psychological time and space. Although physically separated from a place by thousands of miles, you can mentally live

in the distant place as though it were
here. Your imagination can easily trans-
form winter into summer, New York
into Florida, and so on. Whether the
object of your desire be near or far, results will be the same. Subjectively,
the object of your desire is never far off;
its intense nearness makes it remote from
observation of the senses. It dwells in
consciousness, and consciousness is closer
than breathing and nearer than hands
and feet.

Consciousness is the one and only
reality. All phenomena are formed of
the same substance vibrating at different
rates. All is consciousness modified by
belief. Out of consciousness I as man
came, and to consciousness I as man
return. In consciousness all states exist

subjectively, and are awakened to their objective existence by belief. The only thing that prevents us from making a successful subjective impression on one at a great distance, or transforming *there* into *here,* is our habit of regarding space as an obstacle.

A friend a thousand miles away is rooted in your consciousness through your fixed ideas of him. To think of him and represent him to yourself inwardly in the state you desire him to be, confident that this subjective image is as true as though it were already objectified, awakens in him a corresponding state which he must objectify. The results will be as obvious as the cause was hidden. The subject will express the awakened state within him and remain

unaware of the true cause of his action.
Your illusion of free will is but ignorance
of the causes which make you act.
Prayers depend upon your attitude of
mind for their success and not upon the
attitude of the subject. The subject has
no power to resist your controlled
subjective ideas of him unless the state
affirmed by you to be true of him is a
state he is incapable of wishing as true of
another. In that case, it returns to you,
the sender, and will realize itself in you.
Provided the idea is acceptable, success
depends entirely on the operator not upon
the subjects who, like compass needles on
their pivots, are quite indifferent as to
what direction you choose to give them.
If your fixed idea is not subjectively
accepted by the one toward whom it is

directed, it rebounds to you from whom it came. "Who is he that will harm you, if ye be followers of that which is good? I have been young, and now am old; yet have I not seen the righteous forsaken, nor his seed begging bread." "There shall no evil happen to the just." Nothing befalls us that is not of the nature of ourselves.

A person who directs a malicious thought to another will be injured by its rebound if he fails to get subconscious acceptance of the other. "As ye sow, so shall ye reap." Furthermore, what you can wish and believe of another can be wished and believed of you, and you have no power to reject it if the one who desires it for you accepts it as true of you. The only power to reject a subjective word is to be incapable of wishing a similar state of another—to give presupposes the ability to receive. The possibility to impress an idea upon another mind presupposes the ability of that mind to receive that impression. Fools exploit the world; the wise transfigure it. It is the highest wisdom to know that in the living universe there is no destiny other than that created out of the imagination of man. There is no influence outside of the mind of man.

"Whatsoever things are lovely, whatsoever things are of good report; if there be any virtue, and if there be any praise, think on these things." Never accept as true of others what you would not want to be true of you. To awaken a state within another it first must be awake within you. The state you would transmit to another can be transmitted only if it is believed by you. Therefore, to give is to receive. You cannot give what you do not have and you have only what you believe. So to believe a state as true of another not only awakens that state within the other but it makes it alive within you. You are what you believe.

"Give and ye shall receive, full measure, pressed down and running over." Giving is simply believing, for what you truly believe of others you awaken within them. The vibratory state transmitted by your belief persists until it awakens its corresponding vibration in him of whom it is believed. But before it can be transmitted it must first be awake within the consciousness of the transmitter. Whatever is awake within your consciousness, you are. Whether the belief pertains to self or another does not matter, for the believer is defined by the sum total of his beliefs or subconscious assumptions.

"As a man thinketh in his heart"—in the deep subconscious of himself—"so is he." Disregard appearances and subjectively affirm as true that which you wish to be true. This awakens in you the tone of the state affirmed which in turn realizes itself in you and in the one of whom it is affirmed. Give and ye shall receive. Beliefs invariably awaken what they affirm. The world is a mirror wherein everyone sees himself reflected. The objective world reflects the beliefs of the subjective mind.

Some people are self-impressed best by

visual images, others by mental sounds, and still others by mental actions. The form of mental activity which allows the whole power of your attention to be focused in one chosen direction is the one to cultivate, until you can bring all to play on your objective at the same time.

Should you have some difficulty in understanding the terms, "visual images," "mental sounds" and "mental actions," here is an illustration that should make their meanings clear: A imagines he sees a piece of music, knowing nothing at all about musical notations. The impression in his mind is a purely *visual image*. B imagines he sees the same piece, but he can read music and can imagine how it would sound when played on the piano; that imagination is *mental sound*. C also reads music and is a pianist; as he reads, he imagines himself playing the piece. The imaginary action is *mental action*.

The visual images, mental sounds and mental actions are creations of your imagination, and though they appear to come from without, they actually come from within yourself. They move as if moved by another but are really launched by your own spirit from the magical storehouse of imagination. They are projected into space by the same vibratory law that governs the sending of a voice or picture. Speech and images are projected not as speech or images but as vibratory correlates. Subjective mind vibrates according to the modifications it undergoes by the thought and feelings of the operator. The visible state created is the effect of the subjective vibrations. A feeling is always accompanied by a corresponding vibration, that is, a change in expression or sensation in the operator.

There is no thought or feeling without expression. No matter how motionless you appear to be if you reflect with any degree of intensity, there is always an execution of slight muscular movements. The eye, though shut, follows the movements of the imaginary objects and the pupil is dilated or contracted according to the brightness or the remoteness of those objects; respiration is accelerated or slowed, according to the course of your thoughts; the muscles contract correspondingly to your mental movements.

This change of vibration persists until it awakens a corresponding vibration in the subject, which vibration then expresses itself in a physical fact. "And the word was made flesh." Energy, as you see in the case of radio, is transmitted and received in a "field," a place where changes in space occur. The field and energy are one and inseparable. The field or subject becomes the embodiment of the word or energy received. The thinker and the thought, the operator and the subject, the energy and the field are one. Were you still enough to hear the sound of your beliefs you would know what is meant by "the music of the spheres." The mental sound you hear in prayer as coming from without are really produced by yourself. Self-observation will reveal this fact. As the music of the spheres is defined as the harmony heard by the gods alone, and is supposed to be produced by the movements of the celestial spheres, so, too, is the harmony you subjectively hear for others heard by you alone and is produced by the movements of your thoughts and feelings in the true kingdom or "heaven within you."

6. *Good Tidings*

"HOW beautiful upon the mountains are the feet of him that bringeth good tidings, that publisheth peace, that bringeth good tidings of good, that publisheth salvation."

A very effective way to bring good tidings to another is to call before your mind's eye the subjective image of the person you wish to help and have him affirm that he has done that which you desired him to do. Mentally hear him tell you that he has done it. This awakens within him the vibratory correlate of the state affirmed, which vibration persists until its mission is accomplished. It does not matter what it is you desire to have done, or whom you select to do it. As soon as you subjectively affirm that it is done, results follow. Failure can result only if you fail to accept the truth of your assertion or if the state affirmed would not be desired by the subject for himself or another. In the latter event, the state would realize itself in you, the operator.

The seemingly harmless habit of "talking to yourself" is the most fruitful form of prayer. A mental argument with the subjective image of another is the surest way to pray for an argument. You are asking to be offended by the other when you objectively meet. He is compelled to act in a manner displeasing to you, unless before the meeting you countermand or modify your order by subjectively affirming a change.

Unfortunately, man forgets his sub-

jective arguments, his daily mental conversations with others, and so is at a loss
for an explanation of the conflicts and
misfortunes of his life. As mental arguments produce conflicts, so happy mental
conversations produce corresponding visible states of good tidings. Man creates
himself out of his own imagination.

If the state desired is for yourself and
you find it difficult to accept as true what
your senses deny, call before your mind's
eye the subjective image of a friend and
have him mentally affirm that you are already that which you desire to be. This
establishes in him, without his conscious
consent or knowledge, the subconscious
assumption that you are that which he
mentally affirmed, which assumption, because it is unconsciously assumed, will

persist until it fulfills its mission. Its mission is to awaken in you its vibratory correlate, which vibration when awakened in you realizes itself as an objective fact.

Another very effective way to pray for oneself is to use the formula of Job who found that his own captivity was removed as he prayed for his friends. Fix your attention on a friend and have the imaginary voice of your friend tell you that he is, or has that which is comparable to that which you desire to be or have. As you mentally hear and see him, feel the thrill of his good fortune and sincerely wish him well. This awakens in him the corresponding vibration of the state affirmed, which vibration must then objectify itself as a physical fact. You will discover the truth of the statement, "Blessed are the merciful for they shall receive mercy." "The quality of mercy is twice blessed—it blesses him who taketh and him who giveth." The good you subjectively accept as true of others will not only be expressed by them, but a full share will be realized by you.

Transformations are never total. Force A is always transformed into more than a force B. A blow with a hammer produces not only a mechanical concussion, but also heat, electricity, a sound, a magnetic change and so on. The vibratory correlate in the subject is not the entire transformation of the sentiment communicated. The gift transmitted to another is like the divine measure, pressed down, shaken together and running over, so that

after the five thousand are fed from the
five loaves and two fish, twelve baskets
full are left over.

7. *The Greatest Prayer*

IMAGINATION is the beginning of creation. You imagine what you desire, and then you believe it to be true. Every dream could be realized by those self-disciplined enough to believe it. People are what you choose to make them; a man is according to the manner in which you look at him. You must look at him with different eyes before he will objectively change. "Two men looked from the prison bars, one saw the mud and the other saw the stars." Centuries ago, Isaiah asked the question: "Who is blind, but my servant, or deaf, as my messenger that I sent?" "Who is blind as he that is perfect, and blind as the Lord's servant?" The perfect man judges not after appearances, but judges righteously. He sees others as he desires them to be; he hears only what he wants to hear. He sees only the good in others. In him is no condemnation for he transforms the world with his seeing and hearing.

"The king that sitteth on the throne scattereth the evil with his eye." Sympathy for living things—agreement with human limitations—is not in the consciousness of the king because he has learned to separate their false concepts from their true being. To him poverty is but the sleep of wealth. He does not see caterpillars, but painted butterflies to be; not winter, but summer sleeping; not man in want, but Jesus sleeping. Jesus of Nazareth, who scattereth the evil with his eye, is asleep in the imagination of every man, and out of his own imagination must man awaken him by subjectively affirming "I AM Jesus." Then and only then will he see Jesus, for man can only see what is awake within himself. The holy womb is man's imagination. The holy child is that conception of himself which fits Isaiah's definition of perfection. Heed the words of St. Augustine, "Too late have I loved thee, for behold thou wert within and it was without that I did seek thee." It is to your own consciousness that you must turn as to the only reality. There, and there alone, you awaken that which is asleep. "Though Christ a thousand times in Bethlehem be born, if He is not born in thee thy soul is still forlorn."

Creation is finished. You call your creation into being by feeling the reality of the state you would call. A mood attracts its affinities but it does not create what it attracts. As sleep is called by *feeling* "I am sleepy," so, too, is Jesus Christ called by the *feeling,* "I am Jesus Christ." Man sees only himself. Nothing befalls man that is not of the nature of himself. People emerge out of the mass betraying their close affinity to your moods as they are engendered. You meet them seemingly by accident but find they are intimates of your moods. Because your moods continually externalize themselves you could prophesy from your moods, that you, without search, would soon meet certain characters and encounter certain conditions. Therefore call the perfect one into being by living in the feeling, "I am Christ," for Christ is the one concept of

self through which can be seen the un-
veiled realities of eternity.

Our behavior is influenced by our subconscious assumption respecting our own
social and intellectual rank and that of
the one we are addressing. Let us seek
for and evoke the greatest rank, and the
noblest of all is that which disrobes man
of his mortality and clothes him with un-
curbed immortal glory. Let us assume
the feeling, "I am Christ," and our whole
behavior will subtly and unconsciously
change in accordance with that assumption.

Our subconscious assumptions continually externalize themselves that others
may consciously see us as we subconsciously see ourselves, and tell us by their
actions what we have subconsciously as-

sumed ourselves to be. Therefore let us assume the feeling, "I AM Christ," until our conscious claim becomes our subconscious assumption that "We all with open face beholding as in a glass the glory of the Lord are changed into the same image from glory to glory." Let God awake and His enemies be destroyed. There is no greater prayer for man.

FEELING
IS THE SECRET

NEVILLE

"Of making many books there is no end."—*Eccl.* 11:12.

"He that would perfect himself in any art whatsoever, let him betake himself to the reading of some sure and certain work upon his art many times over; for to read many books upon your art produceth confusion rather than learning."—*Old saying.*

Foreword

THIS book is concerned with the art of realizing your desire. It gives you an account of the mechanism used in the production of the visible world. It is a small book but not slight. There is a treasure in it, a clearly defined road to the realization of your dreams.

Were it possible to carry conviction to another by means of reasoned arguments and detailed instances this book would be many times its size. It is seldom possible, however, to do so by means of written statements or arguments since to the suspended judgment it always seems plausible to say that the author was dishonest or deluded, and, therefore, his evidence was tainted.

Consequently, I have purposely omitted all arguments and testimonials, and simply challenge the open-minded reader to practice the law of consciousness as revealed in this book. Personal success will prove far more convincing than all the books that could be written on the subject.

—NEVILLE.

I. *Law and Its Operation*

THE world, and all within it, is man's conditioned consciousness objectified. Consciousness is the cause as well as the substance of the entire world. So it is to consciousness that we must turn if we would discover the secret of creation.

Knowledge of the law of consciousness and the method of operating this law will enable you to accomplish all you desire in life. Armed with a working knowledge of this law, you can build and maintain an ideal world.

Consciousness is the one and only reality, not figuratively but actually. This reality may for the sake of clarity be likened unto a stream which is divided into two parts, the conscious and the sub-

71

conscious. In order to intelligently operate the law of consciousness it is necessary to understand the relationship between the conscious and the subconscious. The conscious is personal and selective; the subconscious is impersonal and non-selective. The conscious is the realm of effect; the subconscious is the realm of cause. These two aspects are the male and female divisions of consciousness. The conscious is male; the subconscious is female. The conscious generates ideas and impresses these ideas on the subconscious; the subconscious receives ideas and gives form and expression to them.

By this law — first conceiving an idea and then impressing the idea conceived on the subconscious—all things evolve out of consciousness; and without this sequence there is not anything made that is made. The conscious impresses the subconscious while the subconscious expresses all that is impressed upon it.

The subconscious does not originate ideas but accepts as true those which the conscious mind feels to be true and in a way known only to itself objectifies the accepted ideas. Therefore, through his power to imagine and feel and his freedom to choose the idea he will entertain, man has control over creation. Control of the subconscious is accomplished through control of your ideas and feelings.

The mechanism of creation is hidden in the very depth of the subconscious, the female aspect or womb of creation. The subconscious transcends reason and is independent of induction. It contemplates a feeling as a fact existing within itself and on this assumption proceeds to give expression to it. The creative process begins with an idea and its cycle runs its course as a feeling and ends in a volition to act.

Ideas are impressed on the subconscious through the medium of feeling. No idea can be impressed on the subconscious until it is felt, but once felt—be it good, bad or indifferent—it must be expressed. Feeling is the one and only medium through which ideas are conveyed to the subconscious. Therefore, the man who does not control his feeling may easily impress the subconscious with undesirable states. By control of feeling is not meant restraint or suppression of your feeling, but rather the disciplining of self to imagine and entertain only such feeling as contributes to your happiness. Control of your feeling is all important to a full and happy life. Never entertain an undesirable feeling nor think sympathetically about wrong in any shape or form. Do not dwell on the imperfection of yourself or others. To do so is to impress the subconscious with these limitations. What you do not want done unto you, do not feel that it is done unto you or another. This is the whole law of a full and happy life. Everything else is commentary.

Every feeling makes a subconscious impression and unless it is counteracted by a more powerful feeling of an opposite nature must be expressed. The dominant

of two feelings is the one expressed. *I
am healthy* is a stronger feeling than *I
will be healthy.* To feel *I will be* is to
confess *I am not; I am* is stronger than
I am not. What you feel you are always
dominates what you feel you would like
to be; therefore, to be realized the wish
must be felt as a state that is rather than
a state that is not.

Sensation precedes manifestation and
is the foundation upon which all manifestation rests. Be careful of your moods
and feelings, for there is an unbroken
connection between your feelings and
your visible world. Your body is an
emotional filter and bears the unmistak-
able marks of your prevalent emotions.
Emotional disturbances, especially suppressed emotions, are the causes of all

disease. To feel intensely about a wrong without voicing or expressing that feeling, is the beginning of disease—dis-ease — in both body and environment. Do not entertain the feeling of regret or failure for frustration or detachment from your objective results in disease.

Think feelingly only of the state you desire to realize. Feeling the reality of the state sought and living and acting on that conviction is the way of all seeming miracles. All changes of expression are brought about through a change of feeling. A change of feeling is a change of destiny. All creation occurs in the domain of the subconscious. What you must acquire, then, is a reflective control of the operation of the subconscious, that is, control of your ideas and feelings.

Chance or accident is not responsible for the things that happen to you, nor is predestined fate the author of your fortune or misfortune. Your subconscious impressions determine the conditions of your world. The subconscious is not selective; it is impersonal and no respecter of persons. The subconscious is not concerned with the truth or falsity of your feeling. It always accepts as true that which you feel to be true. Feeling is the assent of the subconscious to the truth of that which is declared to be true. Because of this quality of the subconscious there is nothing impossible to man. Whatever the mind of man can conceive and *feel* as true, the subconscious can and must objectify. Your feelings create the pattern from which your world is fashioned, and a change of feeling is a change of pattern.

The subconscious never fails to express that which has been impressed upon it. The moment it receives an impression it begins to work out the ways of its expression. It accepts the feeling impressed upon it, *your feeling,* as a fact existing within itself and immediately sets about to produce in the outer or objective world the exact likeness of that feeling. The subconscious never alters the accepted beliefs of man. It out-pictures them to the last detail whether or not they are beneficial.

To impress the subconscious with the desirable state you must assume the feeling that would be yours had you already realized your wish. In defining your objective you must be concerned only with the objective itself. The manner of expression or the difficulties involved are not to be considered by you. To think feelingly on any state impresses it on the subconscious. Therefore, if you dwell on difficulties, barriers or delay, the subconscious, by its very non-selective nature, accepts the feeling of difficulties and obstacles as your request and proceeds to produce them in your outer world.

The subconscious is the womb of creation. It receives the idea unto itself through the feelings of man. It never changes the idea received, but always gives it form. Hence the subconscious out-pictures the idea in the image and likeness of the feeling received. To feel a state as hopeless or impossible is to impress the subconscious with the idea of failure.

Although the subconscious faithfully serves man it must not be inferred that the relation is that of a servant to a master as was anciently conceived. The ancient prophets called it the slave and servant of man. St. Paul personified it as a "woman" and said: "The woman should be subject to man in everything." The subconscious does serve man and faithfully gives form to his feelings. However, the subconscious has a distinct distaste for compulsion and responds to persuasion rather than to command; consequently, it resembles the beloved wife more than the servant.

"The husband is head of the wife," *Eph.* 5, may not be true of man and woman in their earthly relationship but it is true of the conscious and the subconscious, or the male and female aspects of consciousness. The mystery to which Paul referred when he wrote, "This is a great mystery. . . . He that loveth his wife loveth himself. . . . And they two shall be one flesh," is simply the mystery of consciousness. Consciousness is really one and undivided but for creation's sake it appears to be divided into two.

The conscious (objective) or male aspect truly is the head and dominates the subconscious (subjective) or female aspect. However, this leadership is not that of the tyrant but of the lover. So by assuming the feeling that would be yours were you already in possession of your objective, the subconscious is moved to build the exact likeness of your assumption. Your desires are not subconsciously accepted until you assume the feeling of their reality, for only through feeling is an idea subconsciously accepted and only through this subconscious acceptance is it ever expressed.

It is easier to ascribe your feeling to events in the world than to admit that the conditions of the world reflect your feeling. However, it is eternally true that the outside mirrors the inside. "As within so without." "A man can receive nothing unless it is given him from heaven," and "The kingdom of heaven is within you." Nothing comes from without; all things come from within — from the subconscious. It is impossible for you to see other than the contents of your consciousness. Your world in its every detail is your consciousness objectified. Objective states bear witness of subconscious impressions. A change of impression results in a change of expression.

The subconscious accepts as true that which you feel as true, and because creation is the result of subconscious impressions, you, by your feeling, determine creation. You are already that which you want to be, and your refusal to believe this is the only reason you do not see it. To seek on the outside for that which you do not feel you are is to seek in vain, for we never find that which we want; we find only that which we are. In short, you express and have only that which you are conscious of being or possessing. "To him that hath it is given." Denying the evidence of the senses and appropriating the feeling of the wish fulfilled is the way to the realization of your desire.

Mastery of self—control of your thoughts and feelings—is your highest achievement. However, until perfect self-control is attained so that in spite of appearances you feel all that you want to feel, use *sleep* and *prayer* to aid you in realizing your desired states. These are the two gateways into the subconscious.

2. *Sleep*

SLEEP, the life that occupies one-third of our stay on earth, is the natural door into the subconscious. So it is with sleep that we are now concerned. The conscious two-thirds of our life on earth is measured by the degree of attention we give sleep. Our understanding of and delight in what sleep has to bestow will cause us, night after night, to set out for it as though we were keeping an appointment with a lover.

"In a dream, in a vision of the night, when deep sleep falleth upon men, in slumbering upon the bed; then he openeth the ears of men and sealeth their instruction." *Job* 33. It is in sleep and in prayer, a state akin to sleep, that man enters the subconscious to make his impressions and receive his instructions. In these states the conscious and subconscious are creatively joined. The male and female become one flesh.

Sleep is the time when the male or conscious mind turns from the world of sense to seek its lover or subconscious self. The subconscious — unlike the woman of the world who marries her husband to change him — has no desire to change the conscious, waking state, but loves it as it is and faithfully reproduces its likeness in the outer world of form. The conditions and events of your life are your children formed from the molds of your subconscious impressions in sleep. They are made in the image and likeness of your innermost feeling that they may reveal you to yourself.

"As in heaven so on earth." As in the subconscious so on earth. Whatever you have in consciousness as you go to sleep is the measure of your expression in the waking two-thirds of your life on earth. Nothing stops you from realizing your objective save your failure to feel that you are already that which you wish to be, or that you are already in possession of the thing sought. Your subconscious gives form to your desires only when you *feel* your wish fulfilled.

The unconsciousness of sleep is the normal state of the subconscious. Because all things come from within yourself, and your conception of yourself determines that which comes, you should always feel the wish fulfilled before you drop off to sleep. You never draw out of the deep of yourself that which you want; you always draw that which you are, and you are that which you feel yourself to be as well as that which you feel as true of others.

To be realized, then, the wish must be resolved into the feeling of being or having or witnessing the state sought. This is accomplished by assuming the feeling of the wish fulfilled. The feeling which comes in response to the question "How would I feel were my wish realized?" is the feeling which should monopolize and immobilize your attention as you relax into sleep. You must be in the consciousness of being or having that which you want to be or to have before you drop off to sleep.

Once asleep man has no freedom of choice. His entire slumber is dominated by his last waking concept of self. It follows, therefore, that he should always assume the feeling of accomplishment and satisfaction before he retires in sleep. "Come before me with singing and thanksgiving." "Enter into his gates with thanksgiving and into his courts with praise." Your mood prior to sleep defines your state of consciousness as you enter into the presence of your everlasting lover, the subconscious. She sees you exactly as you feel yourself to be. If, as you prepare for sleep, you assume and maintain the consciousness of success by feeling "I am successful," you must be successful. Lie flat on your back with your head on a level with your body. Feel as you would were you in possession of your wish and quietly relax into unconsciousness.

"He that keepeth Israel shall neither slumber nor sleep." Nevertheless "He giveth his beloved sleep." The subconscious never sleeps. Sleep is the door through which the conscious, waking mind passes to be creatively joined to the subconscious. Sleep conceals the creative act while the objective world reveals it. In sleep man impresses the subconscious with his conception of himself.

What more beautiful description of this romance of the conscious and subconscious is there than that told in the "Song of Solomon"! "By night on my bed I sought him whom my soul loveth. . . . I found him whom my soul loveth; I held him and I would not let him go, until I had brought him into my mother's house, and into the chamber of her that conceived me."

Preparing to sleep, you *feel* yourself into the state of the answered wish, and then relax into unconsciousness. Your realized wish is he whom you seek. By night on your bed you seek the feeling of the wish fulfilled that you may take it with you into the chamber of her that conceived you, into sleep or the subconscious which gave you form, that this wish also may be given expression. This is the way to discover and conduct your wishes into the subconscious. Feel yourself in the state of the realized wish and quietly drop off to sleep.

Night after night you should assume the feeling of being, having and witnessing that which you seek to be, possess and see manifested. Never go to sleep feeling discouraged or dissatisfied. Never sleep in the consciousness of failure. Your subconscious, whose natural state is sleep, sees you as you believe yourself to be, and whether it be good, bad, or indifferent, the subconscious will faithfully embody your belief. As you feel so do you impress her; and she, the perfect lover, gives form to these impressions and outpictures them as the children of her beloved.

"Thou art all fair, my love; there is no spot in thee," is the attitude of mind to adopt before dropping off to sleep. Disregard appearances and feel that things are as you wish them to be, for "He calleth things that are not seen as though they were, and the unseen becomes seen." To assume the *feeling* of satisfaction is to call conditions into being which will mirror satisfaction. "Signs follow, they do not precede." Proof that you are will follow the consciousness that you are; it will not precede it.

You are an eternal dreamer dreaming non-eternal dreams. Your dreams take form as you assume the feeling of their reality. Do not limit yourself to the past. Knowing that nothing is impossible to consciousness begin to imagine states beyond the experiences of the past. Whatever the mind of man can imagine man can realize. All objective (visible) states were first subjective (invisible) states, and you called them into visible states by assuming the feeling of their reality. The creative process is first imagining and then believing the state imagined. Always imagine and expect the best.

The world cannot change until you change your conception of it. "As within so without." Nations as well as people are only what you believe them to be. No matter what the problem is, no matter where it is, no matter whom it concerns, you have no one to change but yourself, and you have neither opponent nor helper in bringing about the change within yourself. You have nothing to do but convince yourself of the truth of that which you desire to see manifested. As soon as you

succeed in convincing yourself of the
reality of the state sought, results follow
to confirm your fixed belief. You never
suggest to another the state which you desire to see him express; instead you convince yourself that he is already that
which you desire him to be.

Realization of your wish is accomplished by assuming the feeling of the
wish fulfilled. You cannot fail unless you
fail to convince yourself of the reality of
your wish. A change of belief is confirmed by a change of expression. Every
night as you drop off to sleep feel satisfied
and spotless, for your subjective lover
always forms the objective world in the
image and likeness of your conception of
it, the conception defined by your feeling.

The waking two-thirds of your life on

earth ever corroborates or bears witness to your subconscious impressions. The actions and events of the day are effects; they are not causes. Free will is only freedom of choice. "Choose ye this day whom ye shall serve" is your freedom to choose the kind of mood you assume; but the expression of the mood is the secret of the subconscious. The subconscious receives impressions only through the feelings of man and in a way known only to itself gives these impressions form and expression. The actions of man are determined by his subconscious impressions. His illusion of free will, his belief in freedom of action, is but ignorance of the causes which make him act. He thinks himself free because he has forgotten the link between himself and the event.

Man awake is under compulsion to express his subconscious impressions. If in the past he unwisely impressed himself, then let him begin to change his thought and feeling, for only as he does so will he change his world. Do not waste one moment in regret, for to think feelingly of the mistakes of the past is to reinfect yourself. "Let the dead bury the dead." Turn from appearances and assume the feeling that would be yours were you already the one you wish to be.

Feeling a state produces that state. The part you play on the world's stage is determined by your conception of yourself. By feeling your wish fulfilled and quietly relaxing into sleep, you cast yourself in a star role to be played on earth tomorrow, and while asleep you are rehearsed and instructed in your part.

The acceptance of the end automatically wills the means of realization. Make no mistake about this. If, as you prepare for sleep, you do not consciously feel yourself into the state of the answered wish, then you will take with you into the chamber of her who conceived you the sum total of the reactions and feelings of the waking day; and while asleep you will be instructed in the manner in which they will be expressed tomorrow. You will rise believing that you are a free agent, not realizing that every action and event of the day is predetermined by your concept of self as you fell asleep. Your only freedom then is your freedom of reaction. You are free to choose how you feel and

react to the day's drama, but the drama —
the actions, events and circumstances of
the day — have already been determined.

Unless you consciously and purposely
define the attitude of mind with which
you go to sleep, you unconsciously go to
sleep in the composite attitude of mind
made up of all feelings and reactions of
the day. Every reaction makes a subconscious impression and, unless counteracted by an opposite and more dominant
feeling, is the cause of future action.

Ideas enveloped in feeling are creative
actions. Use your divine right wisely.
Through your ability to think and feel
you have dominion over all creation.

While you are awake you are a gar-
dener selecting seed for your garden, but
"Except a corn of wheat fall into the

ground and die, it abideth alone; but if it die, it bringeth forth much fruit." Your conception of yourself as you fall asleep is the seed you drop into the ground of the subconscious. Dropping off to sleeep feeling satisfied and happy compels conditions and events to appear in your world which confirm these attitudes of mind.

Sleep is the door into heaven. What you take in as a feeling you bring out as a condition, action, or object in space. So sleep in the feeling of the wish fulfilled. "As in consciousness so on earth."

3. *Prayer*

PRAYER like sleep is also an entrance into the subconscious. "When you pray, enter into your closet, and when you have shut your door, pray to your Father which is in secret and your Father which is in secret shall reward you openly."

Prayer is an illusion of sleep which diminishes the impression of the outer world and renders the mind more receptive to suggestion from within. The mind in prayer is in a state of relaxation and receptivity akin to the feeling attained just before dropping off to sleep.

Prayer is not so much what you ask for, as how you prepare for its reception. "Whatsoever things ye desire, when ye pray believe that you have received them,

and ye shall have them." The only condition required is that you believe that
your prayers are already realized.

Your prayer must be answered if you
assume the feeling that would be yours
were you already in possession of your objective. The moment you accept the wish
as an accomplished fact the subconscious
finds means for its realization. To pray
successfully then, you must yield to the
wish, that is, feel the wish fulfilled.

The perfectly disciplined man is always in tune with the wish as an accomplished fact. He knows that consciousness
is the one and only reality, that ideas and
feelings are facts of consciousness and are
as real as objects in space; therefore he
never entertains a feeling which does not
contribute to his happiness for feelings

are the causes of the actions and circumstances of his life. On the other hand, the undisciplined man finds it difficult to believe that which is denied by the senses and usually accepts or rejects solely on appearances of the senses. Because of this tendency to rely on the evidence of the senses, it is necessary to shut them out before starting to pray, before attempting to feel that which they deny. Whenever you are in the state of mind, "I should like to but I cannot," the harder you try the less you are able to yield to the wish. You never attract that which you want but always attract that which you are conscious of being.

Prayer is the art of assuming the feeling of being and having that which you want. When the senses confirm the ab-

PRAYER

sence of your wish, all conscious effort to
counteract this suggestion is futile and
tends to intensify the suggestion.

Prayer is the art of yielding to the wish
and not the forcing of the wish. Whenever your feeling is in conflict with your
wish, feeling will be the victor. The
dominant feeling invariably expresses
itself. Prayer must be without effort. In
attempting to fix an attitude of mind
which is denied by the senses, effort is
fatal.

To yield successfully to the wish as an
accomplished fact, you must create a
passive state, a kind of reverie or medi-
tative reflection similar to the feeling
which precedes sleep. In such a relaxed
state the mind is turned from the objective
world and easily senses the reality of a

subjective state. It is a state in which you are conscious and quite able to move or open your eyes but have no desire to do so.

An easy way to create this passive state is to relax in a comfortable chair or on a bed. If on a bed, lie flat on your back with your head on a level with your body, close the eyes and imagine that you are sleepy. Feel—I am sleepy, so sleepy, so very sleepy. In a little while a far-away feeling accompanied by a general lassitude and loss of all desire to move envelops you. You feel a pleasant, comfortable rest and not inclined to alter your position, although under other circumstances you would not be at all comfortable. When this passive state is reached, imagine that you have realized your wish — not *how* it was realized—but simply the wish fulfilled. Imagine in picture form what you desire to achieve in life; then feel yourself as having already achieved it. Thoughts produce tiny little speech movements which may be heard in the passive state of prayer as pronouncements from without. However, this degree of passivity is not essential to the realization of your prayers. All that is necessary is to create a passive state and *feel* the wish fulfilled.

All you can possibly need or desire is already yours. You need no helper to give it to you; it is yours now. Call your desires into being by imagining and feeling your wish fulfilled. As the end is accepted you become totally indifferent as to possible failure, for acceptance of the end wills the means to that end. When you emerge from the moment of prayer it is as though you were shown the happy and successful end of a play although you were not shown how that end was achieved. However, having witnessed the end, regardless of any anticlimactic sequence you remain calm and secure in the knowledge that the end has been perfectly defined.

4. *Spirit — Feeling*

"NOT by might, nor by power, but by my spirit, saith the Lord of hosts." Get into the spirit of the state desired by assuming the feeling that would be yours were you already the one you want to be. As you capture the feeling of the state sought, you are relieved of all effort to make it so, for *it is* already so. There is a definite feeling associated with every idea in the mind of man. Capture the feeling associated with your realized wish by assuming the feeling that would be yours were you already in possession of the thing you desire, and your wish will objectify itself.

Faith is feeling. "According to your faith (feeling) be it unto you." You never attract that which you want but always that which you are. As a man is, so does he see. "To him that hath it shall be given and to him that hath not it shall be taken away. . . ." That which you feel yourself to be you are, and you are given that which you are. So assume the *feeling* that would be yours were you already in possession of your wish, and your wish must be realized. "So God created man in his own image, in the image of God created he him." "Let this mind be in you which was also in Christ Jesus, who being in the form of God, thought it not robbery to be equal with God." You are that which you believe yourself to be. Instead of believing *in* God or *in* Jesus — believe you *are* God or you *are* Jesus. "He that believeth on me the works that I do shall he do also" should be "He that believes *as* I believe the works that I do shall he do also." Jesus found it not strange to do the works of God because he believed himself to be God. "I and my Father are one." It is natural to do the works of the one you believe yourself to be. So live in the *feeling* of being the one you want to be and that you shall be.

When a man believes in the value of the advice given him and applies it, he establishes within himself the reality of success.

Freedom for All

A PRACTICAL APPLICATION OF THE BIBLE

NEVILLE

PREFACE

PUBLIC opinion will not long endure a theory which does not work in practice. Today, probably more than ever before, man demands proof of the truth of even his highest ideal. For ultimate satisfaction man must find a principle which is for him a way of life, a principle which he can experience as true.

I believe I have discovered just such a principle in the greatest of all sacred writings, the Bible. Drawn from my own mystical illumination this book reveals the truth buried within the stories of the old and new testaments alike.

Briefly, the book states that consciousness is the one and only reality, that consciousness is the cause and manifestation is the effect. It draws the reader's attention to this fact constantly, that the reader may always keep first things first.

PREFACE

Having laid the foundation that a change of consciousness is essential to bring about any change of expression, this book explains to the reader a dozen different ways to bring about such a change of consciousness.

This is a realistic and constructive principle *that works*. The revelation it contains, if applied, *will set you free*.

1. THE ONENESS OF GOD

"HEAR, O Israel: the Lord our God is one Lord."

Hear, O Israel: Hear, O man made of the very substance of God: You and God are one and undivided! Man, the world and all within it are conditioned states of the unconditioned one, God. You are this one; you are God conditioned as man. All that you believe God to be, you are; but you will never know this to be true until you stop claiming it of another, and recognize this seeming other to be yourself. God and man, spirit and matter, the formless and the formed, the creator and the creation, the cause and the effect, your Father and you are one. This one, in whom all conditioned states live and move and have their being, is your I AM, your unconditioned consciousness.

Unconditioned consciousness is God, the one and only reality. By unconditioned consciousness is meant a sense of awareness; a sense of knowing *that I AM* apart from knowing *who I AM;* the consciousness of being, divorced from that which I am conscious of being. I AM aware of being man, but I need not be man to be aware of being. Before I became aware of being someone, I, unconditioned awareness, was aware of being, and this awareness does not depend upon being *someone.* I AM self-existent, unconditioned consciousness; I became aware of being someone; and I shall become aware of being someone other than this that I am now aware of being; but I AM eternally aware of being whether I am unconditioned formlessness or I am conditioned form.

As the conditioned state, I (man), might forget *who* I am, or *where* I am, but I cannot forget *that* I AM. This knowing that I AM, this awareness of being, is the only reality. This unconditioned consciousness, the I AM, is that knowing reality in whom all conditioned states—conceptions of myself—begin and end, but which ever remains the unknown knowing being when all the known ceases to be. All that I have ever believed myself to be, all that I now believe myself to be, and all that I shall ever believe myself to be, are but attempts to know myself,—the unknown, undefined reality. This unknown knowing one, or unconditioned consciousness, is my true being, the one and only reality. I AM the unconditioned reality conditioned as that which I believe myself to be. I AM the believer limited by my beliefs, the knower defined by the known. The world is my conditioned consciousness objectified. That which I feel and believe to be true of myself is now projected in space as my world. The world —my mirrored self—ever bears witness of the state of consciousness in which I live.

There is no chance or accident responsible for the things that happen to me or the environment in which I find myself. Nor is predestined fate the author of my fortunes or misfortunes. Innocence and guilt are mere words with no meaning to the law of consciousness, except as they reflect the state of consciousness itself.

The consciousness of guilt calls forth condemnation. The consciousness of lack produces poverty. Man everlastingly objectifies the state of consciousness in which he abides but he has somehow or other become confused in the interpretation of the law of cause and effect. He has forgotten that it is the *inner* state which is the cause of the outer manifestation,—"As within so without," and in his forgetfulness he believes that an outside God has his own peculiar reason for doing things, such reasons being beyond the comprehension of mere man; or he believes that people are suffering because of past mistakes which have been forgotten by the conscious mind; or, again, that blind chance alone plays the part of God.

One day man will realize that his own I Amness is the God he has been seeking throughout the ages, and that his own sense of awareness—his consciousness of being—is the one and only reality.

The most difficult thing for man to really grasp is this: That the "I amness" in himself is God. It is his true being or father state, the only state he can be sure of. The son, his conception of himself, is an illusion. He always knows that he *is,* but that *which* he is, is an illusion created by himself (the father) in an attempt at self-definition.

This discovery reveals that all that I have believed God to be I AM. "I AM the resurrection and the life," is a statement of fact concerning my consciousness, for my consciousness resurrects or makes visibly alive that which I am conscious of being. "I AM the door . . . all that ever came before me are thieves and robbers," shows me that my consciousness is the one and only entrance into the world of expression; that by assuming the consciousness of being or possessing the thing which I desire to be or possess is the only way by which I can become it or possess it; that any attempt to express this desirable state in ways other than by assuming the consciousness of being or possessing it, is to be robbed of the joy of expression and possession. "I AM the beginning and the end," reveals my consciousness as the cause of the birth and death of all expression. "I AM hath sent me," reveals my consciousness to be the Lord which sends me into the world in the image and likeness of that which I am conscious of being to live in a world composed of all that I am conscious of. "I AM the Lord, and there is no God beside me," declares my consciousness to be the one and only Lord and beside my consciousness there is no God. "Be still and know that I AM God," means that I should still the mind and know that consciousness is God. "Thou shalt not take the name of the Lord thy God in vain." "I AM the Lord: that is my name." Now that you have discovered your I AM, your consciousness to be God, do not claim anything to be true of yourself that you would not claim to be true of God, for in defining yourself you are defining God. That which you are conscious of being is that which you have named God. God and man are one. You and your Father are one. Your unconditioned consciousness, or I AM, and that which you are conscious of being, are one. The conceiver and the conception are one. If your conception of yourself is less than that which you claim as true of God, you have robbed God, the Father, because you (the son or conception) bear witness of the Father or conceiver. ˉDo not take the magical name of God, I AM, in vain for you will not be held guiltless; you must express all that you claim yourself to be. Name God by consciously defining yourself as your highest ideal.

2. THE NAME OF GOD

IT cannot be stated too often that consciousness is the one and only reality, for this is the truth that sets man free. This is the foundation upon which the whole structure of biblical literature rests. The stories of the Bible are all mystical revelations written in an Eastern symbolism which reveals to the intuitive the secret of creation and the formula of escape. The Bible is man's attempt to express in words the cause and manner of creation. Man discovered that his consciousness was the cause or creator of his world, so he proceeded to tell the story of creation in a series of symbolical stories known to us today as the Bible.

To understand this greatest of books you need a little intelligence and much intuition—intelligence enough to enable you to read the book, and intuition enough to interpret and understand what you read. You may ask why the Bible was written symbolically. Why was it not written in a clear, simple style so that all who read it might understand it? To these questions I reply that all men speak symbolically to that part of the world which differs from their own. The language of the West is clear to us of the West, but it is symbolic to the East; and vice versa. An example of this can be found in the Easterner's instruction: "If thine hand offend thee cut it off." He speaks of the hand, not as the hand of the body, but as any form of expression, and thereby he warns you to turn from that expression in your world which is offensive to you. At the same time the man of the West would unintentionally mislead the man of the East by saying: "This bank is on the rocks," for the expression "on the rocks" to the Westerner is equivalent to bankruptcy while a rock to an Easterner is a symbol of faith and security. "I will liken him unto a wise man, which built his house upon a rock; and the rain descended, and the floods came, and the winds blew and beat upon that house; and it fell not; for it was founded upon a rock."

To really understand the message of the Bible you must bear in mind that it was written by the Eastern mind and therefore cannot be taken literally by those of the West. Biologically, there is no difference between the East and the West. Love and hate are the same; hunger and thirst are the same; ambition and desire are the same; but the technique of expression is vastly different.

The first thing you must discover if you would unlock the secret of the Bible, is the meaning of the symbolic name of the creator which is known to all as Jehovah. This word "Jehovah" is composed of the four Hebrew letters—JOD HE VAU HE. The whole secret of creation is concealed within this name. The first letter JOD represents the absolute state or consciousness unconditioned; the sense of undefined awareness; that all inclusiveness out of which all creation or conditioned states of consciousness come. In the terminology of today JOD is I AM, or unconditioned consciousness.

The second letter HE represents the only begotten Son, a desire, an imaginary state. It symbolizes an idea; a defined subjective state or clarified mental picture.

The third letter VAU symbolizes the act of unifying or joining the conceiver (JOD), the consciousness desiring to the conception (HE), the state desired, so that the conceiver and the conception become one. Fixing a mental state, consciously defining yourself as the state desired, impressing upon yourself the fact that you are now that which you imagined or conceived as your objective, is the function of VAU. It nails or joins the consciousness desiring to the thing desired. The cementing or joining process is accomplished subjectively by feeling the reality of that which is not yet objectified.

The fourth letter (HE) represents the objectifying of this subjective agreement. The JOD HE VAU makes man or the manifested world (HE), in the image and likeness of itself, the subjective conscious state. So the function of the final HE is to objectively bear witness to the subjective state JOD HE VAU. Conditioned consciousness continually objectifies itself on the screen of space. The world is the image and likeness of the subjective conscious state which created it. The visible world of itself can do nothing; it only bears record of its creator, the subjective state. It is the visible son (HE) bearing witness of the invisible Father, Son and Mother—JOD HE VAU—a Holy Trinity which can only be seen when made visible as man or manifestation.

Your unconditioned consciousness (JOD) is your I AM, which visualizes or images a desirable state (HE), and then becomes conscious of being the state imaged by feeling and believing itself to be the imagined state. The conscious union between you who desire and that which you desire to be, is made possible through the VAU, or your capacity to feel and believe. Believing is simply living in the feeling of actually being the state imagined—by assuming the consciousness of being the state desired. The subjective state symbolized as JOD HE VAU then objectifies itself as HE, thereby completing the mystery of the creator's name and nature, JOD HE VAU HE (Jehovah). JOD is to be aware; HE is to be aware of something; VAU is to be aware as, or to be aware of being that which you were only aware of. The second HE is your visible objectified world which is made in the image and likeness of the JOD HE VAU, or that which you are aware of being.

"And God said, Let us make man in our image, after our likeness." Let us, JOD HE VAU, make the objective manifestation (HE) in our image, the image of the subjective state. The world is the objectified likeness of the subjective conscious state in which consciousness abides. This understanding that consciousness is the one and only reality is the foundation of the Bible. The stories of the Bible are attempts to reveal in symbolic language this secret of creation as well as to show man the one formula of escape from all of his own creations. This is the true meaning of the name of Jehovah, the name by which all things are made and without which there is nothing made that is made. First, you are aware; then you become aware of something; then you become aware as that which you were aware of; then you behold objectively that which you are aware of being.

3. THE LAW OF CREATION

LET us take one of the stories of the Bible and see how the prophets and writers of old revealed the story of creation by this strange Eastern symbolism. We all know the story of Noah and the Ark; that Noah was chosen to create a new world after the world was destroyed by the flood. The Bible tells us that Noah had three sons, Shem, Ham and Japheth. The first son is called Shem, which means name. Ham, the second son, means warm, alive. The third son is called Japheth, which means extension. You will observe that Noah and his three sons Shem, Ham and Japheth contain the same formula of creation as does the divine name of JOD HE VAU HE. Noah, the Father, the conceiver, the builder of a new world is equivalent to the JOD, or unconditioned consciousness, I AM. Shem is your desire; that which you are conscious of; that which you *name* and define as your objective, and is equivalent to the second letter in the divine name (HE). Ham is the warm, live state of feeling, which joins or binds together consciousness desiring and the thing desired, and is therefore equivalent to the third letter in the divine name, the VAU. The last son, Japheth, means extension, and is the extended or objectified state bearing witness of the subjective state and is equivalent to the last letter in the divine name, HE.

You are Noah, the knower, the creator. The first thing you beget is an idea, an urge, a desire, the word, or your first son Shem (name). Your second son Ham (warm, alive) is the secret of FEELING by which you are joined to your desire subjectively so that you, the consciousness desiring, become conscious of being or possessing the thing desired. Your third son, Japheth, is the confirmation, the visible proof that you know the secret of creation. He is the extended or objectified state bearing witness of the invisible or subjective state in which you abide.

In the story of Noah it is recorded that Ham saw the secrets of his Father, and because of his discovery he was made to serve his brothers, Shem and Japheth. Ham, or feeling, is the secret of the Father, your I AM, for it is through feeling that the consciousness desiring is joined to the thing desired. The conscious union or mystical marriage is made possible only through feeling. It is feeling which performs this heavenly union of Father and son, Noah and Shem, unconditioned consciousness and conditioned consciousness. By performing this service, feeling automatically serves Japheth, the extended or expressed state, for there can be no objectified expression unless there is first a subjective impression. To feel the presence of the thing desired, to subjectively actualize a state by impressing upon yourself, through feeling, a definite conscious state is the secret of creation. Your present objectified world is Japheth which

133

was made visible by Ham. Therefore Ham serves his brothers Shem and Japheth, for without feeling which is symbolized as Ham, the idea or thing desired (Shem) could not be made visible as Japheth.

The ability to feel the unseen, the ability to actualize and make real a definite subjective state through the sense of feeling is the secret of creation, the secret by which the word or unseen desire is made visible,—is made flesh. "And God calleth things that be not as though they were." Consciousness calls things that are not seen as though they were, and it does this by first defining itself as that which it desires to express, and second by remaining within the defined state until the invisible becomes visible. Here is the perfect working of the law according to the story of Noah. This very moment you are aware of being. This awareness of being, this *knowing that you are,* is Noah, the creator.

Now with Noah's identity established as your

own consciousness of being, name something that you would like to possess or express; define some objective (Shem), and with your desire clearly defined, close your eyes and *feel* that you have it or are expressing it. Don't question how it can be done; simply *feel* that you have it. Assume the attitude of mind that would be yours if you were already in possession of it so that you feel that it is done. Feeling is the secret of creation. Be as wise as Ham and make this discovery that you too may have the joy of serving your brothers Shem and Japheth; the joy of making the word or name flesh.

4. THE SECRET OF FEELING

THE secret of feeling or the calling of the invisible into visible states is beautifully told in the story of Isaac blessing his second son Jacob in the belief, based solely upon feeling, that he was blessing his first son Esau. It is recorded that Isaac, who was old and blind, felt that he was about to leave this world and wishing to bless his first son Esau before he died, sent Esau hunting for savory venison with the promise that upon his return from the hunt he would receive his father's blessing.

Now Jacob, who desired the birthright or right to be born through the blessing of his father, overheard his blind father's request for venison and his promise to Esau. So, as Esau went hunting for the venison, Jacob killed and dressed a kid of his father's flock.

Placing the skins upon his smooth body to give him the feel of his hairy and rough brother Esau, he brought the tastily prepared kid to his blind father Isaac. And Isaac who depended solely upon his sense of feel mistook his second son Jacob for his first son Esau, and pronounced his blessing on Jacob! Esau on his return from the hunt learned that his smooth-skinned brother Jacob had supplanted him so he appealed to his father for justice; but Isaac answered and said, "Thy brother came with subtlety and hath taken away thy blessing. I have made him thy Lord, and all his brethren have I given to him for servants."

Simple human decency should tell man that this story cannot be taken literally. There must be a message for man hidden somewhere in this treacherous and despicable act of Jacob! The hidden message, the formula of success buried in this story was intuitively revealed to the writer in this manner. Isaac, the blind father, is your consciousness; your awareness of being.

Esau, the hairy son, is your present objectified world—the rough or sensibly felt; the present moment; the present environment; your present conception of yourself; in short, the world you know by reason of your objective senses. Jacob, the smooth-skinned lad, the second son, is your desire or subjective state; an idea not yet embodied; a subjective state which is perceived and sensed but not objectively known or seen; a point in time and space removed from the present. In short, Jacob is your defined objective. The smooth-skinned Jacob—or subjective state seeking embodiment or the right of birth —when properly felt or blessed by his father (when consciously felt and fixed as real), becomes objectified; and in so doing he supplants the rough, hairy Esau, or the former objectified state. Two things cannot occupy a given place at one and the same time, and so as the invisible is made visible, the former visible state vanishes.

Your consciousness is the cause of your world. The conscious state in which you abide determines the kind of world in which you live. Your present concept of yourself is now objectified as your environment, and this state is symbolized as Esau, the hairy, or sensibly felt; the first son. That which you would like to be or possess is symbolized as your second son, Jacob, the smooth-skinned lad who is not yet seen but is subjectively sensed and felt, and will, if properly touched, supplant his brother Esau, or your present world.

Always bear in mind the fact that Isaac, the father of these two sons, or states, is blind. He does not see his smooth-skinned son Jacob; he only feels him. And through the sense of feeling he actually believes Jacob, the subjective, to be Esau, the real, the objectified. You do not see your desire objectively; you simply sense it (feel it) subjectively. You do not grope in space after a desirable state. Like Isaac, you sit still and send your first son hunting by removing your attention from your objective world. Then in the absence of your first son, Esau, you invite the desirable state, your second son, Jacob, to come close so that you may feel it. "Come close, my son, that I may feel you." First, you are aware of it in your immediate environment; then you draw it closer and closer and closer until you sense it and feel it in your immediate presence so that it is real and natural to you.

"If two of you shall agree on earth as touching on any point that they shall ask, it shall be done for them of my Father which is in heaven." The two agree through the sense of feel; and the agreement is established on earth—is objectified; is made real. The two agreeing are Isaac and Jacob—you and that which you desire; and the agreement is made solely on the sense of feeling. Esau symbolizes your present objectified world whether it be pleasant or otherwise. Jacob symbolizes any and every desire of your heart. Isaac symbolizes your true self—with your eyes closed to the present world—in the act of sensing and feeling yourself to be or to possess that which you desire to be or to possess. The secret of

Isaac—this sensing, feeling state—is simply the act of mentally separating the sensibly felt (your present physical state) from the insensibly felt (that which you would like to be). With the objective senses tightly shut Isaac made, and you can make the insensibly felt (the subjective state) seem real or sensibly known; for faith is knowledge.

Knowing the law of self-expression, the law by which the invisible is made visible, is not enough. It must be applied; and this is the method of application.

First: Send your first son Esau—your present objectified world or problem—hunting. This is accomplished simply by closing your eyes and taking your attention away from the objectified limitations. As your senses are removed from your objective world, it vanishes from your consciousness or goes hunting.

Second: With your eyes still closed and your attention removed from the world round about you, consciously fix the natural time and place for the realization of your desire.

With your objective senses closed to your present environment you can sense and feel the reality of any point in time or space, for both are psychological and can be created at will. It is vitally important that the natural time-space condition of Jacob, that is, the natural time and place for the realization of your desire be first fixed in your consciousness. If Sunday is the day on which the thing desired is to be realized, then Sunday must be fixed in consciousness now. Simply begin to feel that it is Sunday until the quietness and naturalness of Sunday is consciously established. You have definite associations with the days, weeks, months and seasons of the year. You have said time and again— "Today feels like Sunday, or Monday, or Saturday; or this feels like Spring, or Summer, or Fall, or Winter." This should convince you that you have definite, conscious impressions that you associate with the days, weeks, and seasons of the year. Then because of these associations you can select any desirable time, and by recalling the conscious impression associated with such time, you can make a subjective reality of that time now.

Do the same with space. If the room in which you are seated is not the room in which the thing desired would be naturally placed or realized, feel yourself seated in the room or place where it would be natural. Consciously fix this time-space impression before you start the act of sensing and feeling the nearness, the reality, and the possession of the thing desired. It matters not whether the place desired be ten thousand miles away or only next door, you must fix in consciousness the fact that right where you are seated is the desired place. You do not make a mental journey; you collapse space. Sit quietly where you are and make "thereness"—"hereness." Close your eyes and feel that the very place where you are is the place desired; feel and sense the reality of it until you are consciously impressed with this fact, for your knowledge of this fact is based solely on your subjective sensing.

Third: In the absence of Esau (the problem) and with the natural time-space established, you invite Jacob (the solution) to come and fill this space—to come and supplant his brother. In your imagination see the thing desired. If you cannot visualize it, sense the general outline of it; contemplate it. Then mentally draw it close to you. "Come close, my son, that I may feel you." Feel the nearness of it; feel it to be in your immediate presence; feel the reality and solidity of it; feel it and see it naturally placed in the room in which you are seated; feel the thrill of actual accomplishment, and the joy of possession.

Now open your eyes. This brings you back to the objective world—the rough or sensibly felt world. Your hairy son Esau has returned from the hunt and by his very presence tells you that you have been betrayed by your smooth-skinned son Jacob,—the subjective, psychologically felt. But, like Isaac, whose confidence was based upon the knowledge of this changeless law, you too will say—"I have made him thy Lord and all his brethren have I given to him for servants." That is, even though your problem appears fixed and real, you have felt the subjective, psychological state to be real to the point of receiving the thrill of that reality; you have experienced the secret of creation for you have felt the reality of the subjective.

You have fixed a definite psychological state which in spite of all opposition or precedent will objectify itself, thereby fulfilling the name of Jacob—the supplanter.

Here are a few practical examples of this drama.

First: The blessing or making a thing real. Sit in your living room and name a piece of furniture, rug or lamp that you would like to have in this particular room. Look at that area of the room where you would place it if you had it.

145

Close your eyes and let all that now occupies
that area of the room vanish. In your imagination see this area as empty space—there is absolutely nothing there. Now begin to fill this
space with the desired piece of furniture; sense
and feel that you have it in this very area.
Imagine you are seeing that which you desired
to see. Continue in this consciousness until you
feel the thrill of possession.

Second: The blessing or the making of a
place real. You are now seated in your apartment in New York City, contemplating the joy
that would be yours if you were on an ocean
liner sailing across the great Atlantic. "I go to
prepare a place for you. And if I go and prepare a place for you, I will come again, and receive you unto myself: that where I am there ye
may be also." Your eyes are closed; you have
consciously released the New York apartment
and in its place you sense and feel that you are
on an ocean liner. You are seated in a deck
chair; there is nothing round you but the vast

Atlantic. Fix the reality of this ship and ocean so that in this state you can mentally recall the day when you were seated in your New York apartment dreaming of this day at sea. Recall the mental picture of yourself seated there in New York dreaming of this day. In your imagination see the memory picture of yourself back there in your New York apartment. If you succeed in looking back on your New York apartment without consciously returning there, then you have successfully prepared the reality of this voyage. Remain in this conscious state feeling the reality of the ship and the ocean; feel the joy of this accomplishment—then open your eyes. You have gone and prepared the place; you have fixed a definite psychological state and where you are in consciousness there you shall be in body also.

Third: The blessing or making real of a point in time. You consciously let go of this day, month or year, as the case may be, and you imagine that it is now that day, month or year which you desire to experience. You sense and feel the reality of the desired time by impressing upon yourself the fact that it is now accomplished. As you sense the naturalness of this time, you begin to feel the thrill of having fully realized that which before you started this psychological journey in time you desired to experience at this time.

With the knowledge of your power to bless you can open the doors of any prison—the prison of illness or poverty or of a humdrum existence. "The Spirit of the Lord God is upon me; because the Lord hath anointed me to preach good tidings unto the meek; he hath sent me to bind up the broken-hearted, to proclaim liberty to the captives, and the opening of the prison to them that are bound."

5. THE SABBATH

"SIX days shall work be done, but on the seventh day there shall be to you an holy day, a Sabbath of rest to the Lord."

These six days are not twenty-four-hour periods of time. They symbolize the psychological moment a definite subjective state is fixed. These six days of work are subjective experiences, and consequently cannot be measured by sidereal time, for the real work of fixing a definite psychological state is done in consciousness. The time spent in consciously defining yourself as that which you desire to be is the measure of these six days. A change of consciousness is the work done in these six creative days; a psychological adjustment, which is measured not by sidereal time but by actual (subjective) accomplishment. Just as a life in retrospect is measured not by years but by the content of those years, so too is this psychological interval measured,—not by the time spent in making the adjustment but by the accomplishment of that interval.

The true meaning of six days of work (creation) is revealed in the mystery of the VAU, which is the sixth letter in the Hebrew alphabet, and the third letter in the divine name—JOD HE VAU HE. As previously explained in the mystery of the name of Jehovah, VAU means to nail or join. The creator is joined to his creation through feeling; and the time that it takes you to fix a definite feeling is the true measure of these six days of creation. Mentally separating yourself from the objective world and attaching yourself through the secret of feeling to the subjective state is the function of the sixth letter of the Hebrew alphabet, VAU, or the six days of work.

There is always an interval between the fixed impression, or subjective state, and the outward expression of that state. This interval is called the Sabbath. The Sabbath is the mental rest which follows the fixed psychological state; it is the result of your six days of work. "The Sabbath was made for man." This mental rest which follows a successful conscious impregnation is the period of mental pregnancy; a period which is made for the purpose of incubating the manifestation. It was made for the manifestation; the manifestation was not made for it. Automatically you keep the Sabbath a day of rest—a period of mental rest—if you succeed in accomplishing your six days of work. There can be no Sabbath, no seventh day, no period of mental rest, until the six days are over,—until the psychological adjustment is accomplished and the mental impression is fully made.

Man is warned that if he fails to keep the Sabbath, if he fails to enter into the rest of God he will also fail to receive the promise—he will fail to realize his desires. The reason for this is simple and obvious. There can be no mental rest

until a conscious impression is made. If a man
fails to fully impress upon himself the fact that
he now has that which heretofore he desired to
possess, he will continue to desire it, and therefore he will not be mentally at rest or satisfied.
If, on the other hand, he succeeds in making this
conscious adjustment so that upon emerging
from the period of silence or his subjective six
days of work, he knows by his feeling that he
has the thing desired, then he automatically enters the Sabbath or the period of mental rest.
Pregnancy follows impregnation. Man does not
continue desiring that which he has already acquired. The Sabbath can be kept as a day of
rest only after man succeeds in becoming conscious of being that which before entering the
silence he desired to be.

The Sabbath is the result of the six days of
work. The man who knows the true meaning
of these six work days realizes that the observ-
ance of one day of the week as a day of physical
quietness is not keeping the Sabbath. The peace

and the quiet of the Sabbath can be experienced only when man has succeeded in becoming conscious of being that which he desires to be. If he fails to make this conscious impression he has missed the mark; he has sinned, for to sin is to miss the mark—to fail to achieve one's objective; a state in which there is no peace of mind. "If I had not come and spoken unto them, they had not had sin." If man had not been presented with an ideal state toward which to aim, a state to be desired and acquired, he would have been satisfied with his lot in life and would never have known sin. Now that man knows that his capacities are infinite, knows that by working six days or by making a psychological adjustment he can realize his desires, he will not be satisfied until he achieves his every objective. He will, with the true knowledge of these six work days, define his objective and set about becoming conscious of being it. When this conscious impression is made it is automatically followed by a period of mental rest, a period the mystic calls the Sabbath, an interval in which the conscious impression will be gestated and physically expressed. The word will be made flesh. But that is not the end! This Sabbath or rest which will be broken by the embodiment of the idea will sooner or later give way to another six days of work as man defines another objective and begins anew the act of defining himself as that which he desires to be.

Man has been stirred out of his sleep through the medium of desire, and can find no rest until he realizes his desire. But before he can enter into the rest of God, or keep the Sabbath, before he can walk unafraid and at peace, he must become a good spiritual marksman and learn the secret of hitting the mark or working six days— the secret by which he lets go the objective state and adjusts himself to the subjective. This secret was revealed in the divine name Jehovah, and again in the story of Isaac blessing his son Jacob. If man will apply the formula as it is revealed in these Bible dramas he will hit a spiritual bull's-eye every time, for he will know that the mental rest or Sabbath is entered only as he succeeds in making a psychological adjustment.

The story of the crucifixion beautifully dramatizes these six days (psychological period) and the seventh day of rest. It is recorded that it was the custom of the Jews to have someone released from prison at the feast of the Passover; and that they were given the choice of having released unto them either Barabbas the robber, or Jesus the Saviour. And they cried, "Release Barabbas." Whereupon Barabbas was released and Jesus was crucified.

It is further recorded that Jesus the Saviour was crucified on the sixth day, entombed or buried on the seventh day, and resurrected on the first day. The saviour in your case is that which would save you from that which you are now conscious of being, while Barabbas the thief is your present conception of yourself which robs you of that which you would like to be. In defining your saviour you define that which would save you and not *how* you would be saved. Your saviour or desire has ways ye know not of; his ways are past finding out. Every problem reveals its own solution. If you were imprisoned you would automatically desire to be free. Freedom, then, is the thing that would save you. It is your saviour.

Having discovered your saviour the next step in this great drama of the resurrection is to release Barabbas, the robber—your present concept of yourself—and to crucify your saviour, or fix the consciousness of being or having that which would save you. Barabbas represents your present problem. Your saviour is that which would free you from this problem. You release Barabbas by taking your attention away from your problem—away from your sense of limitation—for it robs you of the freedom that you seek. And you crucify your saviour by fixing a definite psychological state by feeling that you are free from the limitations of the past.

You deny the evidence of the senses and begin
to feel subjectively the joy of being free. You
feel this state of freedom to be so real that you
too cry out—"I am free!" "It is finished." The
fixing of this subjective state—the crucifixion
—takes place on the sixth day. Before the sun
sets on this day you must have completed the
fixation by feeling—"It is so"—"It is finished."

This subjective knowing is followed by the
Sabbath or mental rest. You will be as one
buried or entombed for you will know that no
matter how mountainous the barriers, how im-
passable the walls appear to be, your crucified
and buried saviour (your present subjective fixation) will resurrect himself. By keeping the
Sabbath a period of mental rest, by assuming the
attitude of mind that would be yours if you
were already visibly expressing this freedom, you
will receive the promise of the Lord, for the
word will be made flesh,—the subjective fixation will embody itself. "And God did rest the

seventh day from all his works." Your consciousness is God resting in the knowledge that —"It is well"—"It is finished." And your objective senses shall confirm that it is so for the day shall reveal it.

6. HEALING

THE formula for the cure of leprosy as revealed in the fourteenth chapter of Leviticus is most illuminating when viewed through the eyes of a mystic. This formula can be prescribed as the positive cure of any disease in man's world, be it physical, mental, financial, social, moral,—anything. It matters not about the nature of the disease or its duration, for this formula can be successfully applied to any and all of them.

Here is the formula as it is recorded in the book of Leviticus. "Then shall the priest command to take for him that is to be cleansed two birds alive and clean . . . and the priest shall command that one of the birds be killed. . . . As for the living bird, he shall take it and shall dip it in the blood of the bird that was killed; and he shall sprinkle upon him that is to be

159

cleansed from the leprosy seven times and shall pronounce him clean and shall let the living bird loose into the open field. . . . And he shall be clean." A literal application of this story would be stupid and fruitless, while on the other hand a psychological application of this formula is wise and fruitful.

A bird is a symbol of an idea. Every man who has a problem or who desires to express something other than that which he is now expressing can be said to have two birds. These two birds or conceptions can be defined as follows: The first bird is your present out-pictured conception of yourself; it is the description which you would give if you were asked to define yourself,—your physical condition, your income, your obligations, your nationality, family, race and so on. Your sincere answer to these questions would necessarily be based solely upon the evidence of your senses and not upon any wishful thinking. This true conception of yourself (based entirely upon the evidences of your senses) defines the first bird. The second bird is defined by the answer you wish you might give to these questions of self-definition. In short, these two birds can be defined as that which you are conscious of being and that which you desire to be.

Another definition of the two birds would be, the first—your present problem regardless of its nature; and the second—the solution to that problem. For example: If you were sick, good health would be the solution. If you were in debt, freedom from debt would be the solution. If you were hungry, food would be the solution. As you have noticed, the *how*, the manner of realizing the solution, is not considered. Only the problem and the solution are considered. Every problem reveals its own solution. For sickness it is health; for poverty it is riches; for weakness it is strength; for confinement it is freedom.

These two states then, your problem and its solution, are the two birds you bring to the priest. You are the priest who now performs the drama of the curing of the man of leprosy—you and your problem. You are the priest; and with this formula for the cure of leprosy you now free yourself from your problem.

First: Take one of the birds (your problem) and kill it by extracting the blood from it. Blood is man's consciousness. "He hath made of one blood all nations of men to dwell on all the face of the earth." Your consciousness is the one and only reality which animates and makes real that which you are conscious of being. So turning your attention away from the problem is equivalent to extracting the blood from the bird. Your consciousness is the one blood which makes all states living realities. By removing your attention from any given state you have drained the lifeblood from that state. You kill or eliminate the first bird (your problem) by removing your attention from it. Into this blood (your consciousness) you dip the live bird (the solution), or that which heretofore you desired to be or possess. This you do by feeling yourself to be the desirable state now.

This dipping of the live bird into the blood of the bird that was killed is similar to the blessing of Jacob by his blind father Isaac. As you recall, blind Isaac could not see his objective world, his son Esau. You, too, are blind to your problem—the first bird—for you have removed your attention from it and therefore you do not see it. Your attention (blood) is now placed upon the second bird (subjective state), and you feel and sense the reality of it.

Seven times you are told to sprinkle the one to be cleansed. This means you must dwell within this new conception of yourself until you mentally enter the seventh day (the Sabbath); until the mind is stilled or fixed in the belief that you are actually expressing or possessing that which you desire to be or to possess. At the seventh sprinkle you are instructed to loose the living bird and pronounce the man clean. As you fully impress upon yourself the fact that you are that which you desire to be, you have symbolically sprinkled yourself seven times; then you are as free as the bird that is loosed. And like the bird in flight which must in a little while return to the earth, so must your subjective impression or claim in a little while embody itself in your world.

This story and all the other stories of the Bible are psychological plays dramatized within the consciousness of man. You are the high priest; you are the leper; you are the birds. Your consciousness or I AM is the high priest; you, the man with the problem, are the leper. The problem, your present concept of yourself, is the bird that is killed; the solution of the problem, what you desire to be, is the living bird that is freed. You re-enact this great drama within yourself by turning your attention away from your problem and placing it upon that which you desire to express. You impress upon yourself the fact that you are that which you desire to be until your mind is stilled in the belief that it is so. Living in this fixed attitude of mind, living in the consciousness that you are now that which you formerly desired to be, is the bird in flight, unfettered by the limitations of the past and moving toward the embodiment of your desire.

7. DESIRE—THE WORD OF GOD

"SO shall my word be that goeth forth out of my mouth; it shall not return unto me void, but it shall accomplish that which I please, and it shall prosper in the thing whereunto I sent it."

God speaks to you through the medium of your basic desires. Your basic desires are words of promise or prophecies that contain within themselves the plan and power of expression.

By basic desire is meant your real objective. Secondary desires deal with the manner of realization. God, your I AM, speaks to you, the conditioned conscious state, through your basic desires. Secondary desires or ways of expression are the secrets of your I AM, the all wise Father. Your Father, I AM, reveals the first and last—"I am the beginning and the end," but never does He reveal the middle or secret of His ways; that is, the first is revealed as the word, your basic desire. The last is its fulfillment—the word made flesh. The second or middle (the plan of unfoldment) is never revealed to man but remains forever the Father's secret.

"For I testify unto every man that heareth the words of the prophecy of this book, if any man shall add unto these things, God shall add unto him the plagues that are written in this book; and if any man shall take away from the words of the book of this prophecy, God shall take away his part out of the book of life."

The words of prophecy spoken of in the book of Revelation are your basic desires which must not be further conditioned. Man is constantly adding to and taking from these words. Not knowing that the basic desire contains the plan and power of expression man is always compromising and complicating his desires. Here is an illustration of what man does to the word of prophecy—his desires.

Man desires freedom from his limitation or

problem. The first thing he does after he defines his objective is to condition it upon something else. He begins to speculate on the manner of acquiring it. Not knowing that the thing desired has a way of expression all of its own he starts planning *how* he is going to get it, thereby adding to the word of God. If, on the other hand, he has no plan or conception as to the fulfillment of his desire, then he compromises his desire by modifying it. He feels that if he will be satisfied with less than his basic desire, then he might have a better chance of realizing it. In doing so he takes from the word of God. Individuals and nations alike are constantly violating this law of their basic desire by plotting and planning the realization of their ambitions; they thereby add to the word of prophecy, or they compromise with their ideals, thus taking from the word of God. The inevitable result is death and plagues or failure and frustration as promised for such violations.

God speaks to man only through the medium

of his basic desires. Your desires are determined by your conception of yourself. Of themselves they are neither good nor evil. "I know and am persuaded by the Lord Christ Jesus that there is nothing unclean of itself but to him that seeth anything to be unclean to him it is unclean." Your desires are the natural and automatic result of your present conception of yourself. God, your unconditioned consciousness, is impersonal and no respecter of persons. Your unconditioned consciousness, God, gives to your conditioned consciousness, man, through the medium of your basic desires that which your conditioned state (your present conception of yourself) believes it needs.

As long as you remain in your present conscious state so long will you continue desiring that which you now desire. Change your conception of yourself and you will automatically change the nature of your desires.

Desires are states of consciousness seeking

embodiment. They are formed by man's consciousness and can easily be expressed by the man who has conceived them. Desires are expressed when the man who has conceived them assumes the attitude of mind that would be his if the states desired were already expressed. Now because desires regardless of their nature can be so easily expressed by fixed attitudes of mind, a word of warning must be given to those who have not yet realized the oneness of life, and who do not know the fundamental truth that consciousness is God, the one and only reality. This warning was given to man in the famous Golden Rule—"Do unto others that which you would have them do unto you."

You may desire something for yourself or you may desire for another. If your desire concerns another make *sure* that the thing desired is acceptable to that other. The reason for this warning is that your consciousness is God, the giver of all gifts. Therefore, that which you feel and believe to be true of another is a gift you have given to him. The gift that is not accepted returns to the giver. Be very sure then that you would love to possess the gift yourself for if you fix a belief within yourself as true of another and he does not accept this state as true of himself, this unaccepted gift will embody itself within your world. Always hear and accept as true of others that which you would desire for yourself. In so doing you are building heaven on earth. "Do unto others as you would have them do unto you" is based upon this law. Only accept such states as true of others that you would willingly accept as true of yourself that you may constantly create heaven on earth. Your heaven is defined by the state of consciousness in which you live, which state is made up of all that you accept as true of yourself and true of others. Your immediate environment is defined by your own conception of yourself plus your convictions regarding others which have not been accepted by them.

Your conception of another which is not his conception of himself is a gift returned to you.

Suggestions, like propaganda, are boomerangs unless they are accepted by those to whom they are sent. So your world is a gift you have given to yourself. The nature of the gift is determined by your conception of yourself *plus* the unaccepted gifts you offered others. Make no mistake about this; law is no respecter of persons. Discover the law of self-expression and live by it; then you will be free. With this understanding of the law, define your desire; know exactly what you want; make certain that it is desirable and acceptable.

The wise and disciplined man sees no barrier to the realization of his desire; he sees nothing to destroy. With a fixed attitude of mind he recognizes that the thing desired is already fully expressed, for he knows that a fixed subjective state has ways and means of expressing itself of which no man knows. "Before they ask I have answered." "I have ways ye know not of." "My ways are past finding out." The undisciplined man, on the other hand, constantly sees opposition to the fulfillment of his desire, and because of this frustration he forms desires of destruction which he firmly believes must be expressed before his basic desire can be realized. When man discovers this law of one consciousness he will understand the great wisdom of the Golden Rule and so he will live by it and prove to himself that the kingdom of heaven is on earth.

You will realize why you should "Do unto others that which you would have them do unto you." You will know why you should live by this Golden Rule because you will discover that it is just good common sense to do so since the rule is based upon life's changeless law and is no respecter of persons. Consciousness is the one and only reality. The world and all within it are states of consciousness objectified. Your world is defined by your conception of yourself *plus* your conception of others which are not their conceptions of themselves.

The story of the Passover is to help you turn your back on the limitations of the present and pass over into a better and freer state. The suggestion to "Follow the man with the pitcher of water" was given to the disciples to guide them to the last supper or the feast of the Passover. The man with the pitcher of water is the eleventh disciple, Simon of Canaan, the disciplined quality of mind which hears only dignified, noble and kindly states. The mind that is disciplined to hear only the good feasts upon good states and so embodies the good on earth. If you, too, would attend the last supper—the great feast of the Passover—then follow this man. Assume this attitude of mind symbolized as the "man with the pitcher of water," and you will live in a world that is really heaven on earth. The feast of the Passover is the secret of changing your consciousness. You turn your attention from your present conception of yourself and assume the consciousness of being that which you want to be, thereby passing from one state to another. This feat is accomplished with the help of the twelve disciples, which are the twelve disciplined qualities of mind.*

* Your Faith is Your Fortune.

8. FAITH

"AND Jesus said unto them, Because of your unbelief; for verily I say unto you, if ye have faith as a grain of mustard seed, ye shall say unto this mountain, remove hence to yonder place; and it shall remove; and nothing shall be impossible unto you."

This faith of a grain of mustard seed has proved a stumbling block to man. He has been taught to believe that a grain of mustard seed signifies a small degree of faith. So he naturally wonders why he, a mature man, should lack this insignificant measure of faith when so small an amount assures success.

"Faith," he is told, "is the substance of things hoped for, the evidence of things not seen." And again, "Through faith . . . the worlds were framed by the word of God, so that things which are seen were not made of things which do appear." Invisible things were made visible. The grain of mustard seed is not the measure of a small amount of faith. On the contrary, it is the absolute in faith. A mustard seed is conscious of being a mustard seed and a mustard seed alone. It is not aware of any other seed in the world. It is sealed in the conviction that it is a mustard seed in the same manner that the spermatozoa sealed in the womb is conscious of being man and only man. A grain of mustard seed is truly the measure of faith necessary to accomplish your every objective; but like the mustard seed you too must lose yourself in the consciousness of being only the thing desired. You abide within this sealed state until it bursts itself and reveals your conscious claim. Faith is feeling or living in the consciousness of being the thing desired; faith is the secret of creation, the VAU in the divine name JOD HE VAU HE; faith is the Ham in the family of Noah; faith is the sense of feeling by which Isaac blessed and made real his son Jacob. By faith God (your consciousness) calleth things that are not seen as though they were and makes them seen.

It is faith which enables you to become conscious of being the thing desired; again, it is faith which seals you in this conscious state until your invisible claim ripens to maturity and expresses itself, is made visible. Faith or feeling is the secret of this appropriation. Through feeling, the consciousness desiring is joined to the thing desired.

How would you feel if you were that which you desire to be? Wear this mood, this feeling that would be yours if you were already that which you desire to be; and in a little while you will be sealed in the belief that you *are*. Then without effort this invisible state will objectify itself; the invisible will be made visible. If you had the faith of a grain of mustard seed you would this day through the magical substance of feeling seal yourself in the consciousness of being that which you desire to be. In this mental stillness or tomblike state you would remain, confident that you need no one to roll away the stone, for all the mountains, stones and inhabitants of earth are as nothing in your sight. That which you now recognize to be true of yourself (this present conscious state) will do according to its nature among all the inhabitants of earth, and none can stay its hand or say unto it, What doest thou? None can stop this conscious state in which you are sealed from embodying itself, nor question its right to be.

This conscious state when properly sealed by faith is a word of God, I AM, for the man so sealed is saying, "I AM so and so;" and the word of God (my fixed conscious state) is spirit and cannot return unto me void but must accomplish whereunto it is sent. God's word (your conscious state) must embody itself that you may know: "I AM the Lord . . . there is no God beside me;" "The word was made flesh and dwelt among us;" and "He sent his word and healed him."

You too can send your word, God's word, and heal a friend. Is there something that you would like to hear of a friend? Define this something that you know he would love to be or to possess. Now with your desire properly defined you have a word of God. To send this word on its way, to speak this word into being, you simply do this: Sit quietly where you are and assume the mental attitude of listening; recall your friend's voice; with this familiar voice established in your consciousness, imagine that you are actually hearing his voice and that he is telling you that he is or has that which you wanted him to be or to have. Impress upon your consciousness the fact that you actually heard him and that he told you what you wanted to hear; feel the thrill of having heard. Then drop it completely. This is the mystic's secret of sending words into expression—of making the word flesh. You form within yourself the word, the thing you want to hear; then you listen, and tell it to yourself. "Speak, Lord, for thy servant heareth." Your consciousness is the Lord speaking through the familiar voice of a friend and impressing on yourself that which you desire to hear. This self-impregnation, the state impressed upon yourself, the word, has ways and means of expressing itself of which no man knows. As you succeed in making the impression you will be unmoved by appearances for this self-impression is sealed as the grain of mustard seed and will in due season mature to its full expression.

9. THE ANNUNCIATION

THE use of a friend's voice to impregnate one's self with a desirable state is beautifully told in the story of the Immaculate Conception.

It is recorded that God sent an angel to Mary to announce the birth of His son. "And the angel said unto her, thou shalt conceive in thy womb, and bring forth a son. Then said Mary unto the angel, How shall this be, seeing I know not a man? And the angel answered and said unto her, The Holy Ghost shall come upon thee, and the power of the highest shall over-shadow thee: therefore also that holy thing which shall be born of thee shall be called the son of God. For with God nothing shall be impossible."

This is the story that has been told for centuries the world over, but man was not told that it was written about himself so he has failed to receive the benefit it was intended to give him. This story reveals the method by which the idea or word was made flesh. God, we are told, germinated or begat an idea, a son, without the aid of another. Then He placed His germinal idea in the womb of Mary with the help of an angel who made the announcement to her and impregnated her with the idea. No simpler method was ever recorded of consciousness impregnating itself than is found in the story of the Immaculate Conception. The four characters in this drama of creation are the Father, the Son, Mary and the Angel. The Father symbolizes your consciousness; the Son symbolizes your desire; Mary symbolizes your receptive attitude of mind; and the Angel symbolizes the method used to make the impregnation. The drama unfolds in this manner. The Father begets a son without the aid of another. You define your objective—you clarify your desire without the help or suggestion of another.

Then the Father selects that angel who is best qualified to bear this message or germinal possibility to Mary. You select the person in your world who would be sincerely thrilled in witnessing the fulfillment of your desire. Then Mary learns through the angel that she has already conceived a son without the aid of man. You assume a receptive attitude of mind, a listening attitude, and imagine you are hearing the voice of the one you have chosen to tell you what you desire to know. Imagine that you hear him tell you that you are and have that which you desire to be and to have. You remain in this receptive state until you feel the thrill of having heard the good and wonderful news. Then like Mary of the story, you go about your business in secret telling no one of this wonderful and immaculate self-impregnation, confident that in due season you will express this impression.

The Father generates the seed or germinal possibility of a son but in a eugenic impregnation; he does not convey the spermatozoa from himself to the womb. He has it borne through another medium. Consciousness desiring is the Father generating the seed or idea. A clarified desire is the perfectly formed seed or the only begotten son. This seed is then carried from the Father (consciousness desiring) to the Mother (consciousness of being and having the state desired). This change in consciousness is accomplished by the angel or imaginary voice of a friend telling you that you have already achieved your objective.

The use of an angel or friend's voice to make a conscious impression is the shortest, safest and surest way to be self-impregnated. With your desire properly defined, you assume an attitude of listening. Imagine you are hearing the voice of a friend; then make him tell you (imagine he is telling you) how lucky and fortunate you are to have fully realized your desire. In this receptive attitude of mind you are receiving the message of an angel; you are receiving the impression that you are and have that which you desire to be and to have. The emotional thrill of having heard that which you desire to hear is the moment of conception. It is the moment you become self-impregnated, the moment you actually *feel* you are now that or have that which heretofore you but desired to be or to possess.

As you emerge from this subjective experience, you, like Mary of the story, will know by your changed attitude of mind that you have conceived a son; that you have fixed a definite subjective state and will in a little while express or objectify this state.

*   *   *

This book has been written to show you *how* to achieve your objectives. Apply the principle expressed herein and all the inhabitants of earth cannot stop you from realizing your desires.

Out of This World

THINKING FOURTH-DIMENSIONALLY

NEVILLE

1. OUT OF THIS WORLD

"And now I have told you before it come to pass, that, when it is come to pass, ye might believe."—John 14:29.

MANY persons, myself included, have observed events before they occurred; that is, before they occurred in this world of three dimensions. Since man can observe an event before it occurs in the three dimensions of space, life on earth must proceed according to plan, and this plan must exist elsewhere in another dimension and be slowly moving through our space.

If the occurring events were not in this world when they were observed, then, to be perfectly logical, they must have been out of this world. And whatever is *there* to be seen before it occurs *here* must be "predetermined" from the point of view of man awake in a three-dimensional world.

Thus the question arises: "Are we able to alter our future?"

My object in writing these pages is to indicate possibilities inherent in man, to show that man can alter his future; but, thus altered, it forms again a deterministic sequence starting from the point of interference—a future that will be consistent with the alteration. The most remarkable feature of man's future is its flexibility. It is determined by his attitudes rather than by his acts. The cornerstone on which all things are based is man's concept of himself. He acts as he does and has the experiences that he does, because his concept of himself is what it is, and for no other reason. Had he a different concept of self, he would act differently. A change of concept of self automatically alters his future; and a change in any term of his future series of experiences reciprocally alters his concept of self. Man's assumptions which he regards as insignificant produce effects that are considerable; therefore man should revise his estimate of an assumption, and recognize its creative power.

All changes take place in consciousness. The future, although prepared in every detail in advance, has several outcomes. At every moment of our lives we have before us the choice of which of several futures we will choose.

There are two actual outlooks on the world possessed by everyone—a natural focus and a spiritual focus. The ancient teachers called the one "the carnal mind," the other "the mind of Christ." We may differentiate them as ordinary waking consciousness—governed by our senses, and a controlled imagination—governed by desire. We recognize these two distinct centers of thought in the statement: "The natural man receiveth not the things of the spirit of God for they are foolishness unto him; neither can he know them for they are spiritually discerned." The natural view confines reality to the moment called *now*. To the natural view, the past and future are purely imaginary. The spiritual view, on the other hand, sees the contents of time. It sees events as distinct and separated as objects in space. The past and future are a present whole to the spiritual view. What is mental and subjective to the natural man is concrete and objective to the spiritual man.

The habit of seeing only that which our senses permit renders us totally blind to what, otherwise, we could see. To cultivate the faculty of seeing the invisible, we should often deliberately disentangle our minds from the evidence of the senses and focus our attention on an invisible state, mentally feeling it and sensing it until it has all the distinctness of reality.

Earnest, concentrated thought focused in a particular direction shuts out other sensations and causes them to disappear. We have but to concentrate on the state desired in order to see it. The habit of withdrawing attention from the region of sensation and concentrating it on the invisible develops our spiritual outlook and enables us to penetrate beyond the world of sense and to see that which is invisible. "For the invisible things of him from the creation of the world are clearly seen."—Romans 1:20. This vision is completely independent of the natural faculties. Open it and quicken it! Without it, these instructions are useless, for "the things of the spirit are spiritually discerned."

A little practice will convince us that we can, by controlling our imagination, reshape our future in harmony with our desire. Desire is the mainspring of action. We could not move a single finger unless we had a desire to move it. No matter what we do, we follow the desire which at the moment dominates our minds. When we break a habit, our desire to break it is greater than our desire to continue in the habit.

The desires which impel us to action are those that hold our attention. A desire is but an awareness of something we lack or need to make our life more enjoyable. Desires always have some personal gain in view, the greater the anticipated gain, the more intense is the desire. There is no absolutely unselfish desire. Where there is nothing to gain there is no desire, and consequently no action.

The spiritual man speaks to the natural man through the language of desire. The key to progress in life and to the fulfillment of dreams lies in ready obedience to its voice. Unhesitating obedience to its voice is an immediate assumption of the wish fulfilled. To desire a state is to have it. As Pascal has said, "You would not have sought me had you not already found me." Man, by assuming the feeling of his wish fulfilled, and then living and acting on this conviction, alters the future in harmony with his assumption.

Assumptions awaken what they affirm. As soon as man assumes the feeling of his wish fulfilled, his four-dimensional self finds ways for the attainment of this end, discovers methods for its realization. I know of no clearer definition of the means by which we realize our desires than to *experience in imagination what we would experience in the flesh were we to achieve our goal.* This experience of the end wills the means. With its larger outlook the four-dimensional self then constructs the means necessary to realize the accepted end.

The undisciplined mind finds it difficult to assume a state which is denied by the senses. Here is a technique that makes it easy to encounter events before they occur, to "call things which are not seen as though they were." People have a habit of slighting the importance of simple things; but this simple formula for changing the future was discovered after years of searching and experimenting. The first step in changing the future is *desire;* that is: define your objective—know definitely what you want. Secondly: construct an event which you believe you would encounter *following* the fulfillment of your desire—an event which implies fulfillment of your desire—something that will have the action of *self* predominant. Thirdly: immobilize the physical body and induce a condition akin to sleep—lie on a bed or relax in a chair and imagine that you are sleepy; then, with eyelids closed and your attention focused on the action you intend to experience in imagination—mentally feel yourself right into the proposed action —imagining all the while that you are actually performing the action here and now. You must always participate in the imaginary action, not merely stand back and look on, but you must feel that you are actually performing the action so that the imaginary sensation is real to you.

It is important always to remember that the proposed action must be one which *follows* the fulfillment of your desire; and, also, you must feel yourself into the action until it has all the vividness and distinctness of reality. For example: suppose you desired promotion in office. Being congratulated would be an event you would encounter following the fulfillment of your desire. Having selected this action as the one you will experience in imagination, immobilize the physical body, and induce a state akin to sleep—a drowsy state—but one in which you are still able to control the direction of your thoughts—a state in which you are attentive without effort. Now, imagine that a friend is standing before you. Put your imaginary hand into his. First feel it to be solid and real, then carry on an imaginary conversation with him in harmony with the action. Do not visualize yourself at a distance in point of space and at a distance in point of time being congratulated on your good fortune. Instead, make elsewhere *here*, and the future *now*. The future event is a reality *now* in a dimensionally larger world; and, oddly enough, *now* in a dimensionally larger world, is equivalent to *here* in the ordinary three-dimensional space of everyday life. The difference between *feeling* yourself in action, here and now, and visualizing yourself in action, as though you were on a motion-picture screen, is the difference between success and failure. The difference will be appreciated if you will now visualize yourself climbing a ladder. Then with eyelids closed imagine that a ladder is right in front of you and *feel* you are actually climbing it.

Desire, physical immobility bordering on sleep, and imaginary action in which self feelingly predominates, *here and now,* are not only important factors in altering the future, but they are essential conditions in consciously projecting the spiritual self. If, when the physical body is immobilized we become possessed of the idea to do something—and imagine that we are doing it *here and now* and keep the imaginary action feelingly going right up until sleep ensues—we are likely to awaken out of the physical body to find ourselves in a dimensionally larger world with a dimensionally larger focus and actually doing what we desired and imagined we were doing in the flesh. But whether we awaken there or not, we are actually performing the action in the fourth-dimensional world, and we will re-enact it in the future, here in the third-dimensional world.

Experience has taught me to restrict the im-

198

aginary action, to condense the idea which is to be the object of our meditation into a single act, and to re-enact it over and over again until it has the feeling of reality. Otherwise, the attention will wander off along an associational track, and hosts of associated images will be presented to our attention. In a few seconds they will lead us hundreds of miles away from our objective in point of space, and years away in point of time. If we decide to climb a particular flight of stairs, because that is the likely event to follow the realization of our desire, then we must restrict the action to climbing that particular flight of stairs. Should our attention wander off, we must bring it back to its task of climbing that flight of stairs and keep on doing so until the imaginary action has all the solidity and distinctness of reality. The idea must be maintained in the field of presentation without any sensible effort on our part. We must, with the minimum of effort, permeate the mind with the feeling of the wish fulfilled.

Drowsiness facilitates change because it favors attention without effort, but it must not be pushed to the stage of sleep, in which we shall no longer be able to control the movements of our attention, but rather a moderate degree of drowsiness in which we are still able to direct our thoughts. A most effective way to embody a desire is to assume the feeling of the wish fulfilled and then, in a relaxed and sleepy state, repeat over and over again, like a lullaby, any short phrase which implies fulfillment of our desire, such as "Thank you" as though we addressed a higher power for having done it for us. If, however, we seek a conscious projection into a dimensionally larger world, then we must keep the action going right up until sleep ensues.

Experience in imagination, with all the distinctness of reality, what would be experienced in the flesh were you to achieve your goal; and you shall, in time, meet it in the flesh as you met it in your imagination. Feed the mind with *premises*—that is, assertions *presumed* to be true, because assumptions, though unreal to the senses, if persisted in, until they have the *feeling of reality,* will harden into facts. To an assumption all means which promote its realization are good. It influences the behavior of all by inspiring in all the movements, the actions, and the words which tend towards its fulfillment.

To understand how man molds his future in harmony with his assumption we must know what we mean by a dimensionally larger world, for it is to a dimensionally larger world that we go to alter our future. The observation of an event before it occurs implies that the event is predetermined from the point of view of man in the three-dimensional world. Therefore, to change the conditions here in the three dimensions of space we must first change them in the four dimensions of space.

Man does not know exactly what is meant by a dimensionally larger world, and would no doubt deny the existence of a dimensionally larger self. He is quite familiar with the three dimensions of length, width and height, and he feels that if there were a fourth dimension, it should be just as obvious to him as the dimensions of length, width and height. A dimension is not a line; it is any way in which a thing can be measured that is entirely different from all other ways. That is, to measure a solid fourth-dimensionally, we simply measure it in any direction except that of its length, width and height.

Is there another way of measuring an object other than those of its length, width and height? Time measures my life without employing the three dimensions of length, width and height. There is no such thing as an instantaneous object. Its appearance and disappearance are measurable. It endures for a definite length of time. We can measure its life span without using the dimensions of length, width and height. Time is definitely a fourth way of measuring an object.

The more dimensions an object has, the more substantial and real it becomes. A straight line, which lies entirely in one dimension, acquires shape, mass and substance by the addition of dimensions. What new quality would time, the fourth dimension, give which would make it just as vastly superior to solids as solids are to surfaces and surfaces are to lines? Time is a medium for changes in experience because all changes take time. The new quality is *changeability*.

Observe that if we bisect a solid, its cross section will be a surface; by bisecting a surface, we obtain a line; and by bisecting a line, we get a point. This means that a point is but a cross section of a line, which is, in turn, but a cross section of a surface, which is, in turn, but a cross section of a solid, which is, in turn, if carried to its logical conclusion, but a cross section of a four-dimensional object.

We cannot avoid the inference that all three-dimensional objects are but cross sections of four-dimensional bodies. Which means: when I meet you, I meet a cross section of the four-dimensional you—the four-dimensional *self* that is not seen. To see the four-dimensional *self* I must see every cross section or moment of your life from birth to death and see them all as coexisting. My focus should take in the entire array of sensory impressions which you have experienced on earth plus those you might encounter. I should see them, not in the order in which they were experienced by you, but as a present whole. Because *change* is the characteristic of the fourth dimension, I should see them in a state of flux as a living, animated whole.

If we have all this clearly fixed in our minds, what does it mean to us in this three-dimensional world? It means that, if we can move along time's length, we can see the future and alter it as we so desire. This world, which we think so solidly real, is a shadow out of which and beyond which we may at any time pass. It is an abstraction from a more fundamental and dimensionally larger world—a more fundamental world abstracted from a still more fundamental and dimensionally larger world—and so on to infinity. The absolute is unattainable by any means or analysis, no matter how many dimensions we add to the world.

Man can prove the existence of a dimensionally larger world simply by focusing his attention on an invisible state and imagining that he sees and feels it. If he remains concentrated in this state, his present environment will pass away, and he will awaken in a dimensionally larger world where the object of his contemplation will be seen as a concrete objective reality. Intuitively I feel that, were he to abstract his thoughts from this dimensionally larger world and retreat still farther within his mind, he would again bring about an externalization of time. He would discover that every time he retreats into his inner mind and brings about an externalization of time, space becomes dimensionally larger. And he would, therefore, conclude that both time and space are serial, and that the drama of life is but the climbing of a multitudinous dimensional time block.

Scientists will one day explain *why* there is a Serial Universe. But in practice *how* we use this Serial Universe to change the future is more important. To change the future, we need only concern ourselves with two worlds in the infinite series, the world we know by reason of our bodily organs, and the world we perceive independently of our bodily organs.

2. ASSUMPTIONS BECOME FACTS

MEN believe in the reality of the external world because they do not know how to focus and condense their powers to penetrate its thin crust. This book has only one purpose—the removing of the veil of the senses—the traveling into another world. To remove the veil of the senses we do not employ great effort; the objective world vanishes by turning our attention away from it.

We have only to concentrate on the state desired in order to mentally see it, but to give it reality so that it will become an objective fact, we must focus attention upon the invisible state until it has the feeling of reality. When, through concentrated attention, our desire appears to possess the distinctness and feeling of reality, we have given it the right to become a visible concrete fact.

If it is difficult to control the direction of your attention while in a state akin to sleep, you may find gazing fixedly into an object very helpful. Do not look at its surface but into and beyond any plain object such as a wall, a carpet, or any other object which possesses depth. Arrange it to return as little reflection as possible. Imagine then that in this depth you are seeing and hearing what you want to see and hear until your attention is exclusively occupied by the imagined state.

At the end of your meditation, when you awake from your "controlled waking dream," you feel as though you had returned from a great distance. The visible world which you had shut out returns to consciousness and by its very presence informs you that you have been self-deceived into believing that the object of your contemplation was real. But, if you know that consciousness is the one and only reality, you will remain faithful to your vision, and by this sustained mental attitude confirm your gift of reality, and prove that you have the power to give reality to your desires that they may become visible concrete facts.

Define your ideal and concentrate your attention upon the idea of identifying yourself with your ideal. Assume the feeling of being it, the feeling that would be yours were you already the embodiment of your ideal. Then live and act upon this conviction. This assumption, though denied by the senses, *if persisted in,* will become fact. You will know when you have succeeded in fixing the desired state in consciousness by simply looking *mentally* at the people you know. In dialogues with yourself you are less inhibited and more sincere than in actual conversations with others, therefore the opportunity for self-analysis arises when you are surprised by your mental conversations with others. If you see them as you formerly saw them, you have not changed your concept of self, for all changes of concepts of self result in a changed relationship to your world.

In your meditation allow others to see you as they would see you were this new concept of self a concrete fact. You always seem to others an embodiment of the ideal you inspire. Therefore, in meditation, when you contemplate others, you must be seen by them mentally as you would be seen by them physically were your concept of self an objective fact; that is, in meditation you imagine that they see you expressing that which you desire to be.

If you assume that you are what you want to be your desire is fulfilled, and in fulfillment all longing is neutralized. You cannot continue desiring what you have already realized. Your desire is not something you labor to fulfill, it is recognizing something you already possess. It is assuming the feeling of *being* that which you desire to be. Believing and being are one. The conceiver and his conception are one, therefore that which you conceive yourself to be can never be so far off as even to be near, for nearness implies separation. "If thou canst believe,

all things are possible to him that believeth."
Being is the substance of things hoped for, the
evidence of things not yet seen. If you assume
that you are what you want to be, then you will
see others as they are related to your assumption.

If, however, it is the good of others that you
desire, then, in meditation, you must represent
them to yourself as already being that which
you desire them to be. It is through desire that
you rise above your present sphere and the road
from longing to fulfillment is shortened as you
experience in imagination what you would
experience in the flesh were you already the
embodiment of the ideal you desire to be.

I have stated that man has at every moment
of time the choice before him which of several
futures he will encounter; but the question
arises: "How is this possible when the experiences
of man, awake in the three-dimensional world,
are predetermined?" as his observation of an
event before it occurs implies. This ability to
change the future will be seen if we liken the

experiences of life on earth to this printed page. Man experiences events on earth singly and successively in the same way that you are now experiencing the words of this page.

Imagine that every word on this page represents a single sensory impression. To get the context, to understand my meaning, you focus your vision on the first word in the upper left-hand corner and then move your focus across the page from left to right, letting it fall on the words singly and successively. By the time your eyes reach the last word on this page you have extracted my meaning. Suppose, however, on looking at the page, with all the printed words thereon equally present, you decided to rearrange them. You could, by rearranging them, tell an entirely different story; in fact, you could tell many different stories.

A dream is nothing more than uncontrolled four-dimensional thinking, or the rearrangement of both past and future sensory impressions. Man seldom dreams of events in the order in which he experiences them when awake. He usually dreams of two or more events which are separated in time, fused into a single sensory impression; or, in his dream, he so completely rearranges his single waking sensory impressions that he does not recognize them when he encounters them in his waking state.

For example: I dreamed that I delivered a package to the restaurant in my apartment building. The hostess said to me, "You can't leave that there"; whereupon, the elevator operator gave me a few letters and as I thanked him for them, he, in turn, thanked me. At this point, the night elevator operator appeared and waved a greeting to me.

The following day, as I left my apartment, I picked up a few letters which had been placed at my door. On my way down I gave the day elevator operator a tip and thanked him for taking care of my mail; whereupon, he thanked me for the tip. On my return home that day I overheard a doorman say to a delivery man,

"You can't leave that there." As I was about to take the elevator up to my apartment, I was attracted by a familiar face in the restaurant, and, as I looked in, the hostess greeted me with a smile. Late that night I escorted my dinner guests to the elevator and as I said good-by to them, the night operator waved good-night to me.

By simply rearranging a few of the single sensory impressions I was destined to encounter, and by fusing two or more of them into single sensory impressions, I constructed a dream which differed quite a bit from my waking experience.

When we have learned to control the movements of our attention in the four-dimensional world, we shall be able to consciously create circumstances in the three-dimensional world. We learn this control through the waking dream, where our attention can be maintained without effort, for *attention minus effort* is indispensable to changing the future. We can, in a controlled waking dream, consciously construct an event which we desire to experience in the three-dimensional world.

The sensory impressions we use to construct our waking dream are present realities displaced in time or the four-dimensional world. All that we do in constructing the waking dream is to select from the vast array of sensory impressions those, which, when they are properly arranged, imply that we have realized our desire. With the dream clearly defined we relax in a chair and induce a state of consciousness akin to sleep—a state, which, although bordering on sleep, leaves us in conscious control of the movements of our attention. When we have achieved that state, we experience in imagination what we would experience in reality were this waking dream an objective fact. In applying this technique to change the future it is important always to remember that the only thing which occupies the mind during the waking dream *is* the waking dream, the predetermined action which implies the fulfillment of our desire. How the waking dream becomes physical fact is not our concern. Our acceptance of the waking dream as physical reality wills the means for its fulfillment.

Let me again lay the foundation of changing the future, which is nothing more than a controlled waking dream.

1. Define your objective—know definitely what you want.

2. Construct an event which you believe you will encounter *following* the fulfillment of your desire—something which will have the action of *self* predominant—an event which implies the fulfillment of your desire.

3. Immobilize the physical body and induce a state of consciousness akin to sleep; then, mentally feel yourself right into the proposed action—imagining all the while that you are actually performing the action *here and now* so that you experience in imagination what you would experience in the flesh were you now to realize your goal.

Experience has convinced me that this is the perfect way to achieve my goal. However, my own many failures would convict me were I to imply that I have completely mastered the movements of my attention. I can, however, with the ancient teacher say: "This one thing I do, forgetting those things which are behind, and reaching forth unto those things which are before, I press toward the mark for the prize."

3. POWER OF IMAGINATION

"Ye shall know the truth, and the truth shall make you free."—John 8:32.

MEN claim that a true judgment must conform to the external reality to which it relates. This means that if I, while imprisoned, suggest to myself that I am free and succeed in believing that I am free, it is true that I believe in my freedom; but it does not follow that I am free for I may be the victim of illusion. But, because of my own experiences, I have come to believe in so many strange things that I see little reason to doubt the truth of things that are beyond my experience.

The ancient teachers warned us not to judge from appearances because, said they, the truth need not conform to the external reality to which it relates. They claimed that we bore false witness if we imagined evil against another —that no matter how real our belief appears to be—how truly it conforms to the external reality to which it relates—if it does not make free the one of whom we hold the belief, it is untrue and therefore a false judgment.

We are called upon to deny the evidence of our senses and to imagine as true of our neighbor that which makes him free. "Ye shall know the truth, and the truth shall make you free." To know the truth of our neighbor we must assume that he is already that which he desires to be. Any concept we hold of another that is short of his fulfilled desire will not make him free and therefore cannot be the truth.

Instead of learning my craft in schools where attending courses and seminars is considered a substitute for self-acquired knowledge, my schooling was devoted almost exclusively to the power of imagination. I sat for hours imagining myself to be other than that which my reason and my senses dictated until the imagined states were vivid as reality—so vivid that passers-by became but a part of my imagination and acted as I would have them. By the power of imagination my fantasy led theirs and dictated to them their behavior and the discourse they held together while I was identified with my imagined state. Man's imagination is the man himself, and the world as imagination sees it is the real world, but it is our duty to imagine all that is lovely and of good report. "The Lord seeth not as man seeth, for man looketh upon the outward appearance, but the Lord looketh upon the heart." "As a man thinketh in his heart so is he."

In meditation, when the brain grows luminous, I find my imagination endowed with the magnetic power to attract to me whatsoever I desire. Desire is the power imagination uses to fashion life about me as I fashion it within myself. I first desire to see a certain person or scene, and then I look *as though I were seeing* that which I want to see, and the imagined state becomes objectively real. I desire to hear, and then I listen *as though I were hearing,* and the imagined voice speaks that which I dictate as though it had initiated the message. I could give you many examples to prove my arguments, to prove that these imagined states do become physical realities; but I know that my examples will awaken in all who have not met the like or who are not inclined towards my arguments, a most natural incredulity. Nevertheless, experience has convinced me of the truth of the statement, "He calleth those things which be not as though they were."—Romans 4:17. For I have, in intense meditation, called things that were not seen as though they were, and the unseen not only became seen, but eventually became physical realities.

By this method—first desiring and then imagining that we are experiencing that which we desire to experience—we can mold the future in harmony with our desire. But let us follow the advice of the prophet and think only the lovely and the good, for the imagination waits on us as indifferently and as swiftly when our nature is evil as when it is good. From us spring forth good and evil. "I have set before thee this day life and good, and death and evil." —Deuteronomy 30:15.

Desire and imagination are the enchanter's wand of fable and they draw to themselves their own affinities. They break forth best when the mind is in a state akin to sleep. I have written with some care and detail the method I use to enter the dimensionally larger world, but I shall give one more formula for opening the door of the larger world. "In a dream, in a vision of the night, when deep sleep falleth upon men, in slumberings upon the bed; Then he openeth the ears of men, and sealeth their instruction."—Job 33:15, 16.

In dream we are usually the servant of our vision rather than its master, but the *internal fantasy* of dream can be turned into an *external reality.* In dream, as in meditation, we slip from this world into a dimensionally larger world, and I know that the forms in dream are not flat two-dimensional images which modern psychologists believe them to be. They are substantial realities of the dimensionally larger world, and I can lay hold of them. I have discovered that, if I surprise myself dreaming, I can lay hold of any inanimate or stationary form of the dream—a chair—a table—a stairway—a tree—and command myself to awake. At the command to awake, while firmly holding on to the object of the dream, I am pulled through myself with the distinct feeling of awakening from dream. I awaken in another sphere holding the object of my dream, to find that I am no longer the servant of my vision but its master, for I am fully conscious and in control of the movements of my attention. It is in this fully conscious state, when we are in control of the direction of thought, that we call things that are not seen as though they were. In this state we call things by wishing and assuming the feeling of our wish fulfilled. Unlike the world of three dimensions where there is an interval between our assumption and its fulfillment, in the dimensionally larger world there is an immediate realization of our assumption. The external reality instantly mirrors our assumption. Here there is no need to wait four months till harvest. We look again as though we saw, and lo and behold, the fields are already white to harvest.

In this dimensionally larger world "Ye shall not need to fight: set yourselves, stand ye still, and see the salvation of the Lord with you."— 2 Chronicles 20:17. And because that greater world is slowly passing through our three-dimensional world, we can by the power of imagination mold our world in harmony with our desire. Look *as though you saw;* listen *as though you heard;* stretch forth your imaginary hand *as though you touched* . . . and your assumptions will harden into facts.

To those who believe that a true judgment must conform to the external reality to which it relates, this will be foolishness and a stumbling-block. But I preach and practice the fixing in consciousness of that which man desires to realize. Experience convinces me that fixed attitudes of mind which do not conform to the external reality to which they relate and are therefore called imaginary—"things which are not"—will, nevertheless, "bring to nought things that are."

I do not wish to write a book of wonders, but rather to turn man's mind back to the one and only reality that the ancient teachers worshiped as God. All that was said of God was in reality said of man's consciousness so we may say, "That, according as it is written, He that glorieth, let him glory in his own consciousness."

No man needs help to direct him in the application of this law of consciousness. "I am" is the self-definition of the absolute. The root out of which everything grows. "I am the vine."

What is your answer to the eternal question, "Who am I?" Your answer determines the part you play in the world's drama. Your answer—that is, your concept of self—need not conform to the external reality to which it relates. This great truth is revealed in the statement, "Let the weak say, I am strong."— Joel 3:10.

Look back over the good resolutions with which many past new years are encumbered. They lived a little while and then they died. Why? Because they were severed from their root. Assume that you are that which you want to be. Experience in imagination what you would experience in the flesh were you already that which you want to be. Remain faithful to your assumption, so that you define yourself as that which you have assumed. Things have no life if they are severed from their roots, and our consciousness, our "I am-

POWER OF IMAGINATION

ness," is the root of all that springs in our world.

"If ye believe not that I am he, ye shall die in your sins."—John 8:24. That is, if I do not believe that I am already that which I desire to be, then I remain as I am and die in my present concept of self. There is no power, outside of the consciousness of man, to resurrect and make alive that which man desires to experience. That man who is accustomed to call up at will whatever images he pleases, will be, by virtue of the power of his imagination, master of his fate. "I am the resurrection, and the life: he that believeth in me, though he were dead, yet shall he live."—John 11:25. "Ye shall know the truth, and the truth shall make you free."

227

4. NO ONE TO CHANGE BUT SELF

"And for their sakes I sanctify myself, that they also might be sanctified through the truth."—John 17:19.

THE ideal we serve and strive to attain could never be evolved from us were it not potentially involved in our nature.

It is now my purpose to retell and to emphasize an experience of mine printed by me two years ago. I believe these quotations from "THE SEARCH" will help us to understand the operation of the law of consciousness, and show us that we have no one to change but self.

"Once in an idle interval at sea I meditated on "the perfect state," and wondered what I would be, were I of too pure eyes to behold iniquity, if to me all things were pure and were I without condemnation. As I became lost in this fiery brooding, I found myself lifted above the dark environment of the senses. So intense was feeling I felt myself a being of fire dwelling in a body of air. Voices as from a heavenly chorus, with the exaltation of those who had been conquerors in a conflict with death, were singing, "He is risen—He is risen," and intuitively I knew they meant me.

Then I seemed to be walking in the night. I soon came upon a scene that might have been the ancient Pool of Bethesda for in this place lay a great multitude of impotent folk—blind, halt, withered—waiting not for the moving of the water as of tradition, but waiting for me. As I came near, without thought or effort on my part they were, one after the other, molded as by the Magician of the Beautiful. Eyes, hands, feet—all missing members—were drawn from some invisible reservoir and molded in harmony with that perfection which I felt springing within me. When all were made perfect, the chorus exulted, "It is finished." Then the scene dissolved and I awoke.

I know this vision was the result of my intense meditation upon the idea of perfection, for my meditations invariably bring about union with the state contemplated. I had been so completely absorbed within the idea that for a while I had become what I contemplated, and the high purpose with which I had for that moment identified myself drew the companionship of high things and fashioned the vision in harmony with my inner nature. The ideal with which we are united works by association of ideas to awaken a thousand moods to create a drama in keeping with the central idea.

My mystical experiences have convinced me that there is no way to bring about the outer perfection we seek other than by the transformation of ourselves. As soon as we succeed in transforming ourselves, the world will melt magically before our eyes and reshape itself in harmony with that which our transformation affirms.

In the divine economy nothing is lost. We

cannot lose anything save by descent from the sphere where the thing has its natural life. There is no transforming power in death and, whether we are here or there, we fashion the world that surrounds us by the intensity of our imagination and feeling, and we illuminate or darken our lives by the concepts we hold of ourselves. Nothing is more important to us than our conception of ourselves, and especially is this true of our concept of the dimensionally greater One within us.

Those who help or hinder us, whether they know it or not, are the servants of that law which shapes outward circumstances in harmony with our inner nature. It is our conception of ourselves which frees or constrains us, though it may use material agencies to achieve its purpose.

Because life molds the outer world to reflect the inner arrangement of our minds, there is no way of bringing about the outer perfection we seek other than by the transformation of ourselves. No help cometh from without; the hills to which we lift our eyes are those of an inner range. It is thus to our own consciousness that we must turn as to the only reality, the only foundation on which all phenomena can be explained. We can rely absolutely on the justice of this law to give us only that which is of the nature of ourselves.

To attempt to change the world before we change our concept of ourselves is to struggle against the nature of things. There can be no outer change until there is first an inner change. As within, so without. I am not advocating philosophical indifference when I suggest that we should imagine ourselves as already that which we want to be, living in a mental atmosphere of greatness, rather than using physical means and arguments to bring about the desired change. Everything we do, unaccompanied by a change of consciousness, is but futile readjustment of surfaces. However we toil or struggle, we can receive no more than our assumptions affirm. To protest against anything which happens to us is to protest against the law of our being and our rulership over our own destiny.

The circumstances of my life are too closely related to my conception of myself not to have been formed by my own spirit from some dimensionally larger storehouse of my being. If there is pain to me in these happenings, I should look within myself for the cause, for I am moved here and there and made to live in a world in harmony with my concept of myself.

Intense meditation brings about a union with the state contemplated, and during this union we see visions, have experiences and behave in keeping with our change of consciousness. This shows us that a transformation of consciousness will result in a change of environment and behavior.

All wars prove that violent emotions are extremely potent in precipitating mental rearrangements. Every great conflict has been followed by an era of materialism and greed in which the ideals for which the conflict ostensibly was waged are submerged. This is inevitable because war evokes hate which impels a descent in consciousness from the plane of the ideal to the level where the conflict is waged. If we would become as emotionally aroused over our ideals as we become over our dislikes, we would ascend to the plane of our ideal as easily as we now descend to the level of our hates.

Love and hate have a magical transforming power, and we grow through their exercise into the likeness of what we contemplate. By intensity of hatred we create in ourselves the character we imagine in our enemies. Qualities die for want of attention, so the unlovely states might best be rubbed out by imagining "beauty for ashes and joy for mourning" rather than by direct attacks on the state from which we would be free. "Whatsoever things are lovely and of good report, think on these things," for we become that with which we are en rapport.

NO ONE TO CHANGE BUT SELF

There is nothing to change but our concept of self. As soon as we succeed in transforming self, our world will dissolve and reshape itself in harmony with that which our change affirms.

RESURRECTION

•

A CONFESSION OF FAITH
IN TERMS OF EXPERIENCE

•

NEVILLE

RESURRECTION

A confession of faith in terms of experience

"Now after John was arrested, Jesus came into Galilee, preaching the gospel of God, and saying, 'The time is fulfilled, and the kingdom of God is at hand; repent, and believe in the gospel.'" Mark 1:14-15

Jesus' ministry began after that of John ended in Judea. "Jesus, when he began his ministry, was about thirty years of age" (Luke 3:23).

The soil of the centuries had been ploughed and harrowed for the gospel of God. And men began to experience God's plan of salvation.

The authors of the gospel of God are anonymous, and all that we can really know about them must be derived from our own experience of scripture. Their authority was not in scripture as a dead written code but in their own experience of scripture. Their gospel was not a new religion but the fulfillment of one as old as the faith of Abraham.

"And the scripture, foreseeing that God would justify the heathen by faith, preached the gospel beforehand to Abraham" (Gal. 3:8). And Abraham believed God and lived in accordance with the preview of the story of salvation that God granted to him.

The unknown authors of the gospel emphasize the fulfillment of scripture in the life of Jesus Christ. Christ in us fulfills the scripture. "Do you not realize that Jesus Christ is in you?" (2 Cor. 13:5). "I have been crucified with Christ; it is no longer I who live, but Christ who lives in me" (Gal. 2:20). "For if we have been united with him in a death like his, we shall certainly be united with him in a resurrection like his" (Rom. 6:4).

The repetition in us, through his indwelling, has been expressed by Johann Scheffler, a seventeenth-century mystic.

> *"Though Christ a thousand times*
> *In Bethlehem be born,*
> *If he's not born in thee,*
> *Thy soul is still forlorn."*

"And he said to them, "O foolish men, and slow of heart to believe all that the prophets have spoken! Was it not necessary that the Christ should suffer these things and enter into his glory? And beginning with Moses and all the prophets, he interpreted to them in all the scriptures the things concerning himself . . . everything written about me in the law of Moses and the prophets and the psalms must be fulfilled. Then he opened their minds to understand the scriptures." (Luke 24:25, 27, 44-45).

"And they read from the book, from the law of God, with interpretation, and they gave the sense, so that the people understood the reading" (Nehemiah 8:8).

The Old Testament is a prophetic blueprint of the life of Jesus Christ. The gospel of God is the revelation of the future granted to Abraham. "Abraham rejoiced that he was to see my day" (John 8:56). It is about the risen Christ. Participation in the life of the age to come depends on God's act of raising the dead. The resurrection of Jesus Christ is God's victory. That we shall be "united wtih him in a resurrection like his" is the promise of God's victory for all.

But before the day of victory, man must

be refined in the furnace of affliction. "I have tried you in the furnace of affliction. For my own sake, for my own sake, I do it, for how should my name be profaned? My glory I will not give to another" (Isaiah 48:10-11). It takes the furnace of affliction to conform us to the image of his Son, and therefore to the image of the Father, for the Father and the Son are one.

"Then came to him all his brothers and sisters and all who had known him efore . . . and comforted him for all the evil that the Lord had brought upon him . . . And the Lord blessed the latter days of Job more than his beginning" (Job 42:11-12). The story of Job is the story of man, the innocent victim of a cruel experiment on the part of God, "And God said, 'Let us make man in our image'" (Gen. 1:26). Yet "I consider that the sufferings of this present time are not worth comparing with the glory that is to be revealed in us" (Rom. 8:18) and that glory is nothing less than the unveiling of God the Father in us, as us.

Nothing can take the place of personal witness to God's plan of salvation. The plan of the mystery is inherent in the creation. What is so prophetically spoken to the world in the Old Testament is realized in one's own personality. All was foretold me but naught could I foresee, but I learned who Jesus Christ really is after the story was re-enacted in me.

The man who has experienced Scripture cannot escape the responsibility of telling its meaning to his fellow men. The unknown writers of the gospel of God were not describing situations and events of the past as historians. Their story of Jesus Christ is their own experience of God's plan of redemption as men who themselves had experienced redemption. They related their own experiences. They are witnesses of the first order testifying to the truth of God's Word, not hesitating to interpret the Old Testament according to their own supernatural experiences.

Having experienced the story of salvation I can add my testimony to theirs and say that all is done as they have told it. Their experiences, thus attested, confront men with the responsibility of accepting or rejecting their interpretation of the Old Testament. Their testimony should be heard and responded to. One must experience Scripture for himself before he can begin to understand how wonderful it is. They give no account of the personal appearance of Jesus, because when the story of salvation is recreated in man, man will know that "I am He." "He who is united to the Lord becomes one spirit with him" (1 Cor. 6:17).

*　*　*

"Being in the form of God, . . . he emptied himself, taking the form of a slave, being born in the likeness of men. And being found in human form he humbled himself and became obedient unto death, even death on the cross" (Phil. 2:6-8) of man. He abdicated his divine form and assumed the form of a slave. He did not merely disguise himself as a slave but became one, subject to all human weaknesses and limitations. God who entered death's door, the human skull, Golgotha, is now the world's Savior. "God is our salvation. Our God is a God of salvation; and to God, the Lord, belongs escape from death" (Ps. 68:19-20). "Unless I die thou canst not live; But if I die I shall arise again and thou with me." The grain of wheat sets out the mystery of life through death. "Unless a grain of wheat falls into the earth and dies,it remains alone; but if it dies, it bears much fruit" (John 12:24). This is the secret of God's plan of salvation. God achieves his purpose by self-limitation, by contraction in order to expand.. God himself enters Death's Door, my skull, and lays down in the Grave with me. And with apologies to William Blake

> "What 'er is done to me I cannot know,
> And if you'll ask me I will swear it so.
> Whether 'tis good or evil none's to blame:
> Only God can take the pride, only God
> the shame."

"And I am sure that he who began a good work in me will bring it to completion at the day of Jesus Christ" (Phil. 1:6). When the image of the unbegotten is formed in me, then He who was so long tightly furled within me, unwinds Himself, and I am He. "No one has ascended into Heaven but he who descended from heaven, the Son of Man" (John 3:13). God himself voluntarily descended into his grave Golgotha, my skull. "I lay down my life, that I may take it again. No one takes it from me, but I lay it down of my own accord" (John 10:17-18). "For your maker is your husband, the Lord of hosts is his name" (Isa. 54:5). And, "He cleaves to his wife and they become one flesh" (Gen. 2:24). For "He who is united to the Lord becomes one Spirit with him" (I Cor. 6:17). "What therefore God has joined together, let not man put asunder" (Mark 10:9). Man is God's emanation, yet his wife till the sleep of death is past. "Rouse thyself! Why sleepest thou O Lord? Awake!" (Ps. 44:23). When he awakes "I am He." God laid Himself down within me to sleep, and as He slept He dreamed a dream; he dreamed that He is I and when He awakes He is I. But how do I know that I am He? Through the revelation of His Son David who in the Spirit calls me Father.

*   *   *

"I am the way, and the truth, and the life; no one comes to the Father, but by me . . . He who has seen me has seen the Father" (John 14:6, 9). Union with the risen Christ is the only way to the Father. Because "Christ and the Father are one" (John 10:30). The way leads through death to life eternal.

Man's search for Christ as the authority which he can trust, which he can respect, to which he can submit is his longing for the Father that lives in him, for that same Father whom the Christ of the Gospel claims to be. The Christ of the Gospel is the Eternal Father in man. This longing for the Father is the cry of man that ends the New Testament. "Come, Lord Jesus!" (Rev. 22:20). "Do you not realize that Jesus Christ is in you?" (2 Cor. 13:5). "And in him the whole fulness of deity dwells bodily?" (Col. 2:9), not figuratively, but genuinely in a body. This is "the mystery hidden for ages and generations . . . which is Christ in you, the hope of glory" (Col. 1:26, 27).

Imperfect knowledge of Jesus has blinded man to the true nature of the Father. The Lord Jesus is God the Father who became man that man might become the Lord Jesus, the Father. Historian's researches cannot yield knowledge of who the Father is. "No one can say 'Jesus is Lord' except by the Holy Spirit" (I Cor. 12:3). Man's goal is to find the Father, but God the Father is made known only through his Son. "No one knows the Son except the Father, and no one knows the Father except the Son and any one to whom the Son chooses to reveal him." (Matt. 11:27). Only the Father and the Son know each other. "Call no man your Father on earth, for you have one Father, who is in Heaven" (Matt. 23:9) and Heaven is "within you" (Luke 17:21).

And David said: "I will tell of the decree of the Lord; He said to me, 'You are my son, today I have begotten you" (Ps. 2:7). David's divine sonship is unique, the only one of its kind and wholly supernatural. He was "born, not of blood nor of the will of the flesh nor of the will of man, but of God" (John 1:13).

The Father will be found by man only in a first person singular, present tense experience when David in the Spirit calls him Father, that is, my Lord. Jesus asked them a question, saying, "What do you think of the Christ? Whose son is he?" They said to him, "The son of David." He said to them, "How is it then that David, in the Spirit, calls him Lord . . . If David thus calls him Lord, how is he his son?" (Matt. 22:41-45).

In Hebrew thought, history consists of all

the generations of men and their experiences fused into one great whole and this concentrated time, into which all the generations are fused, and from which they spring, is called "Eternity." Scripture states that: "God has put eternity into man's mind, yet so that man cannot find out what God has done from the beginning to the end" (Ecc. 3:11). The Hebrew word for "eternity" means also "youth, stripling, young man."

Saul saw David and said to Abner "Whose son is this *youth* . . . Inquire whose son the *stripling* is?" Then turning to David he said: "Whose son are you, *young man?*" And David answered "I am the son of your servant Jesse the Bethemite" (I Sam. 17:55-58). Whose son . . . . ? Note in all the passages (I Sam. 17:55, 56, 58: Matt. 22:42), the inquiry is not about the Son, but about his Father. The Father made known by David is the eternally true Father.

It is in us as persons that God the Father is revealed. David said "I am the son of Jesse." Jesse is any form of the verb to be. David's answer was "I am the son of Him whose name is "I AM." "I am the son of the Lord."

One of the names for God is the name He gave to Moses. "Say to the people of Israel 'I AM has sent me to you'" (Exod. 3:14). He is the Eternal "I AM." God's first revelation of Himself is as "God Almighty" (Exod. 6:3). His second self-revelation is as "The Eternal I AM" (Exod. 3:14). His final revelation of Himself is as "the Father" (John 17). Only the Son can reveal God as Father. "No one (i.e. no human eye, Gr. oudeis) has ever seen God; the only begotten Son, who is in the bosom of the Father, he has made him known" (John 1:18).

It is God Himself, the Eternal I AM, and His only begotten Son, the eternal youth David, who entered man's mind. At the end of his journey through the fires of affliction in this Age of Eternal death, man will find David and exclaim "I have found David . . . He shall cry to me, Thou art my Father, my God, and the Rock of my salvation" (Ps. 89: 20, 26).

I do not reveal myself to myself directly as God or as Jesus Christ, but by implication parallel with Scripture, when David in the Spirit calls me Father. And this wisdom from within is without uncertainty.

"When it pleased God to reveal his Son in me, I did not confer with flesh and blood" (Gal. 1:15-16). The man in whom the Son of God appears finds it difficult to convince others of the reality of the revelation, because these supernatural experiences of Scripture take place in a realm of action too remote from our common experience. The whole drama belongs to a world far more real and vital than that which the intellect inhabits for the historic imagination to understand it.

> *"Oh could I tell ye surely would believe it!*
> *Oh could I only say what I have seen!*
> *How should I tell or how can ye receive it,*
> *How, till he bringeth you where I have*
> *been?"*
>
> F. W. H. Myers

This entrance into the Father-Son relationship is truly by the Grace of God. "For God so loved the world that he gave his only Son" (John 3:16). It was the eternal plan of God to give Himself to man. And it is the Son, calling him Father, who makes him sure that he really is the Father.

When David in the Spirit calls Him Father, he does not lose his distinctive individuality or cease to be the self he was before, but that self now includes a far greater self, which is none other than Jesus Christ whom David in the Spirit called "Lord." Man is heir to a Promise and to a Presence! "Abraham having patiently endured, obtained the promise." (Heb. 6:15). Grace is the final expression of God's love in action which man will experience when the Son is revealed in him, and who in turn reveals man as the Father.

The authority which underlies the story of Jesus Christ is a two-fold witness; the inward testimony of the Father, and the external testimony of Scripture. God Himself came, and comes, into human history in the person of the incarnate Jesus within us. This will be confirmed by the "signs," which will be experienced by man as foretold in Scripture.

"The Father who dwells in me does his works. Believe me that I am in the Father and the Father in me; or else believe me for the sake of the works themselves. Truly, truly, I say to you, he who believes in me will also do the works that I do: and greater works than these will he do, because I go to the Father" (John 14:10-12). "I came from the Father and have come into the world; again, I am leaving the world and going to the Father" (John 16:28). "I and the Father are one" (John 10:30).

The Vision of God is granted to those who have had the revelation of the Father in the life of the incarnate Jesus in them, when the only begotten Son David calls them Father.

Only as the "signs" become our experience is God's purpose—and therefore the Scripture's purpose—fulfilled in us. "Scripture must be fulfilled in me . . . for what is written about me has its fulfillment" (Luke 22:37).

God gave Himself to all of us, to each of us. And it is His only begotten Son David, in the Spirit, calling us Father, who makes us sure that it is really so. "So if the Son makes you free, you will be free indeed" (John 8:36). "And as David returned from the slaughter of the Philistine . . . with the head of the Philistine in his hand. Saul said to him "Whose son are you young man?" (I Sam. 17:57, 58) for he did not know David's father, whom he had promised (I Sam. 17:25) to make free in Israel. The king had promised to make free the father of the man who destroyed the enemy of Israel.

We must not ignore the very personal and supernatural character of God's plan of salvation. The fulfillment of the plan takes place in man; it is inaugurated by the event called "his resurrection from the dead." "We have been born anew . . . through the resurrection of Jesus Christ from the dead" (I Peter 1:3). It is Christ in you—your I AM—who is resurrected. The resurrection marks the beginning of the freeing of Jesus Christ the Father from the body of sin and death, and His return to His divine body of Love, the human form divine. This was the Lord's purpose from the beginning "which he set forth in Christ as a plan for the fullness of time" (Eph. 1:9, 10). "The Lord of hosts has sworn: As I have planned, so shall it be, and as I have purposed, so shall it stand" (Isa. 14.24).

Live and act on the assurance that God has brought his plan to fulfillment and continues to do so. God Himself came, and comes, into human history in the person of Jesus Christ in you, in me, in all. God awoke in the anonymous authors of the gospels, and continues to awake in individual man. Believe their testimony, do not seek new ways of access to a goal already attained.

Perhaps the best description of the unknown writers of the gospel of God is given in the words: "That which . . . we have heard, which we have seen with our eyes, which we have looked upon, and our hands have handled, of the Word of life . . . That which we have seen and heard declare we unto you" (I John 1:1, 3). Faith is not complete till it has become experience. It is essential that those whose eyes have seen and whose hands have handled the Word of life, be sent and be conscious of themselves *as* sent, to declare it to the world.

It is the resurrected Christ, the twice-born man, who says: "Take my yoke upon you, and learn from me . . . and you will find rest for your souls" (Matt. 11:29). He offers his knowledge of Scripture based on his own experience, for that of others based on speculation. Accept his offer. And it will keep you from losing your way among the tangled speculations that pass for religious truth. And show you the only way to the Father.

The man who is sent to preach the gospel of God is first called, and taken in Spirit into the divine assembly where the gods hold judgment. "God has taken his place in the divine council; in the midst of the gods he holds judgment" (Ps. 82:1).

The Hebrew word Elohim is plural, a compound unity, one made up of others. In this sentence it is translated as God and gods. The man who is called is brought before the Elohim, the risen Christ. He is asked to name the greatest thing in the world; he answers in the words of Paul, "faith, hope, and love, these three; but the greatest of these is love" (I Cor. 13:13). At that moment God embraces him, and they fuse and become One. For "he who is united to the Lord becomes one spirit with him" (I Cor. 6:17). "So they are no longer two but one. What therefore God has joined together, let no man put asunder" (Matt. 19:6). Men are called one by one to unite into a single Man, who is God. "The Lord will thresh out the grain, and you will be gathered one by one, O people of Israel" (Isa. 27:12). This union with the risen Christ is baptism with the Holy Spirit. From his baptism with the Holy Spirit to his resurrection, fall the "days of the Messiah," a period of thirty years. During this period, he is so overwhelmingly in love with his mission, as messenger and preacher of the Gospel of God, a gospel which has laid such constraint upon him that he can do no other, feels that "if I preach the gospel, that gives me no ground for boasting. For necessity is laid upon me. Woe to me if I do not preach the gospel!" (I Cor. 9:16). A divine compulsion drives him as it had Jeremiah, who said; "If I say, 'I will not mention him, or speak any more in his name,' there is in my heart as it were a burning fire shut up in my bones, and I am weary with holding it in, and I cannot" (Jer. 20:9).

The end of this thirty year period arrives with such dramatic suddenness that he has no time to observe its coming. "Jesus, when he began his ministry, was about thirty years of age" (Luke 3:23). Now the story of Jesus Christ unfolds in him in a series of the most personal, first person singular, present tense experiences. The entire series of events takes three and a half years. It begins with his resurrection and birth from above.

> *"The dead heard the voice of the child*
> *And began to awake from sleep:*
> *All things heard the voice of the child*
> *And began to awake to life."*

William Blake

While sleeping on his bed and dreaming of the redeemed society of a city "full of boys and girls playing in the streets thereof" (Zech. 8:5), an intense vibration centered at the base of his skull awakens him, "Awake, O sleeper, and arise from the dead, and Christ shall give you light" (Eph. 5:14). As he wakes, he finds that he is not in the room where he fell asleep, but in his own skull (Golgotha). His skull is a completely sealed tomb. He does not know how he got there, but his one consuming desire is to get out. He pushes the base of his skull, and something rolls away leaving a small opening. He pushes his head through the opening and squeezes himself out inch by inch in the same manner that a child is born from his mother's womb. He looks at his body out of which he has just emerged. It is pale of face lying on its back and tossing its head from side to side like one in recovery from a great ordeal. "You will be sorrowful, but your sorrow will turn into joy. When a woman is in travail she has sorrow, because her hour has come; but when she is delivered of the child, she no longer remembers the anguish, for joy that a child is born into the world" (John 16:20, 21).

> *"For there the Babe is born in joy*
> *That was begotten in dire woe;*
> *Just as we Reap in joy the fruit*
> *Which we in bitter tears did sow."*
>
> William Blake

"You must be born from above" (John 3:7). "The Jerusalem above is free, and she is our mother" (Gal. 4:26). The skull that was his tomb became the womb from which he is born anew. The vibration within his skull which roused him from sleep, appears now to be coming from without, it sounds like a great wind. He turns his head in the direction where the wind appears to be. Looking back to where his body was, he is surprised to find that it is gone but in its place sit three men.

This experience that faces him will be the fulfillment of the promise made to Abraham. "And the Lord appeared to him . . . He lifted up his eyes and looked, and behold, three men stood in front of him . . . They said to him, "Where is Sarah your wife?" And he said, "She is in the tent." He said, "I will surely return to you according to the time of life; and Sarah your wife shall have a son . . . Abraham called the name of his son who was born to him . . . Isaac" (he laughs), (Gen. 18:1, 2, 9, 10, 21:3). The three men suddenly appeared, they had not been seen approaching. Abraham does not at once realize the significance of this. They are ordinary men who have chanced to come his way. They too are disturbed by the wind. The youngest of the three is the most disturbed and goes over to investigate the source of the disturbance. His attention is attracted by a babe wrapped in swaddling cloths lying on the floor. He takes the babe in his arms and proclaiming it to be the resurrected man's babe, lays it on the bed. The man then lifts the babe in his arms and says: "How is my sweetheart?" The child *smiles* and the first act comes to an end.

"And in that region there were shepherds out in the field . . . And an angel of the Lord appeared to them . . . And the angel said to them, "Be not afraid; for behold, I bring you good news of a great joy which will come to all the people; for to you is born this day in the city of David a Savior, who is Christ the Lord. And this will be a sign for you: you will find a babe wrapped in swaddling cloths and lying in a manger" (Luke 2:8-12). God is born, for God is called Savior (Isa. 43:3; 45:15: cf. Luke 1.47).

After the revelation, man searches the ancient scriptures for intimations and foreshadowings of his supernatural experience, and finding them there, knows that:

> *"All was foretold me: naught*
> *Could I foresee:*
> *But I learned how the wind would sound*
> *After these things should be."*
>
> Edward Thomas

The unpredictable nature of the wind's course illustrates the spontaneity of the divine birth all the more easily since both in Greek and in Hebrew the word is used both for wind and spirit.

The plan of the Lord is described in the ancient scripture, but it cannot really be known until after it has been experienced by the individual. God has spoken, and what He has foretold is written there for all to understand. But His prophecy appears in a quite different light in prospect from what it is seen to be in retrospect.

Everyone will know that Jesus Christ is the Father in the light of his own experience of the Christian Mystery.

"In these last days he has spoken to us by His Son" (Heb. 1:2). Five months after man is resurrected and born from above, a vibration similar to that which began the first act starts in his head. This time it is centered at the top of his head. It increases in intensity until it explodes. After the explosion he finds himself seated in a modestly furnished room. Leaning against the side of an open door, and looking out on a pastoral scene, is his son David of Biblical fame. He is a youth in his early teens. David addresses him as "My Father." The resurrected man knows that he is David's Father, and David knows that he is his Son. Two men look at

David lustfully and the Father reminds them of his Son's victory over the giant Philistine. And while he is sitting there and contemplating the unearthly beauty of his Son, the second act comes to its end. God the Father gave Himself to man that man might become God the Father. "I will tell of the decree of the Lord: He said to me, "You are my son, today I have begotten you" (Ps. 2:7).

The third act unfolds four months after the Father-Son relationship has been revealed. It is dramatic from beginning to end. A bolt of lightning splits the body of the resurrected man from the top of his skull to the base of his spine. Now the new and living way is opened for him through the curtain, that is, through his body. Revelation is always in personal terms, and the human agents of God's revelation are never suppressed to the level of the impersonal. "Consequently, when he came into the world, he said, "Sacrifices and offerings thou has not desired, but a body hast thou prepared for me; in burnt offerings and sin offerings thou hast taken no pleasure. Then I said 'Lo, I have come to do thy will, O God, as it is written of me in the roll of

the book' " (Heb. 10:5-7. Ps. 40:6-8 is quoted).
God's will is done. God must save and God
alone. At the base of his spine, he sees a pool
of golden liquid light and knows that it is
himself. He now has "confidence to enter the
sanctuary by the blood of Jesus, by the new
and living way which he opened for us through
the curtain, that is, through his flesh" (Heb.
10:19, 20). As he contemplates the pool of
golden liquid light, the blood of God, the
living water, he fuses with it, and knows that
it is himself, his divine Creator and Re-
deemer. Now like a bolt of spiral lightning,
he ascends his spine entering the heavenly
sanctuary of his skull violently. His head
reverberates like thunder. "And as Moses
lifted up the serpent in the wilderness, so
must the Son of man be lifted up" (John 3:14).
"From the days of John the Baptist until now
the kingdom of heaven has been coming
violently, and men of violence take it by
force" (Matt. 11:12). To such men the new
age has come.

Two years and nine months later, fulfilling
the three and a half years of the ministry of
Jesus, the fourth and final act of the drama

of salvation comes to its climax. "And the Holy Spirit descended upon him in bodily form, as a dove, and a voice came from heaven, "Thou art my beloved Son; with thee I am well pleased" (Luke 3:22).

The head of the resurrected one suddenly becomes translucent. Hovering above him, as though floating, a dove with its eyes focused lovingly upon him, descends upon his outstretched hand, he draws her to his face, and the dove smothers him with love, kissing his face, his head and his neck. A woman, daughter of the voice of God says to him: "He loves you" and the drama of salvation comes to its end in him. He is now a son of God, a son of the resurrection. He "cannot die any more, because he is a son of God, being a son of the resurrection" (Luke 20:36). "I and the Father are one" (John 10:30). "I am the root and the offspring of David" (Rev. 22:16). He is the Father of humanity and its offspring. By becoming man, the limit of contraction and opacity, he breaks the shell, and expanding into translucence achieves his purpose. He has "found him of whom Moses in the law and also the prophets wrote"

(John 1:45).

The anonymous authors of the gospel of God are twice-born men, sons of God, sons of the resurrection, who can die no more, having escaped from the body of sin and death. The gospel is the story of God's plan of salvation.

It will be helpful to all readers of the Word of God, to end this confession of faith with a quote from William Blake.

> 'It ought to be understood that the
> Persons, Moses and Abraham, are not
> here meant, but the States Signified
> by those Names, the Individuals
> being representatives or Visions of
> those States as they were reveal'd
> to Mortal Man in the Series of
> Divine Revelations as they are written
> in the Bible: these various States
> I have seen in my Imagination; when
> distant they appear as One Man, but
> as you approach they appear Multitudes
> of Nations."

There is no secular history in the Bible. The Bible is the history of salvation and is wholly supernatural.